HEART OF ENGLAND WALKS

ISBN 1 85284 325 X
A catalogue record for this book is available from the British Library

ABOUT THE AUTHOR

Roger Noyce was born near Stratford-upon-Avon and educated at King Edward VI Grammar School. He has had several books published in the insurance world, and in 1992 won the Morgan Owen Gold Medal for his book *Insurance and The Environment*. Since taking early retirement, Roger has turned his literary skills to his passion for the countryside, and is now the successful author of a number of walking guides.

Roger is an experienced and enthusiastic walker who frequently walks in the Peak District, the Cotswolds and the Heart of England – having walked the Cotswold and the Heart of England Ways on three separate occasions. He has walked Wainwright's Coast to Coast and has completed a 1400 mile 'Walking Way' route from Land's End to John O'Groats. Overseas, Roger has walked in the Alps, the Pyrenees and the Cevennes in France, and holds special memories of the Himalayas and the Inca Trail in Peru. Future plans include walking in Vietnam and, in the UK, Offas' Dyke Path, the Worcestershire Way and the Wychavon Way. He is Chairman of Stratford Group of the Rambler's Association.

Advice to Readers

Readers are advised that while every effort is taken by the author to ensure the accuracy of this guidebook, changes can occur which may affect the contents. It is advisable to check locally on transport, accommodation, shops, etc, but even rights of way can be altered. The publisher would welcome notes of any such changes.

Cover photograph: *View south towards the Herefordshire Beacon*
(Photo courtesy of Tourism and Leisure Services, Great Malvern)

HEART OF ENGLAND WALKS

by

Roger Noyce

CICERONE PRESS
2 POLICE SQUARE, MILNTHORPE
CUMBRIA LA7 7PY
www.cicerone.co.uk

CONTENTS

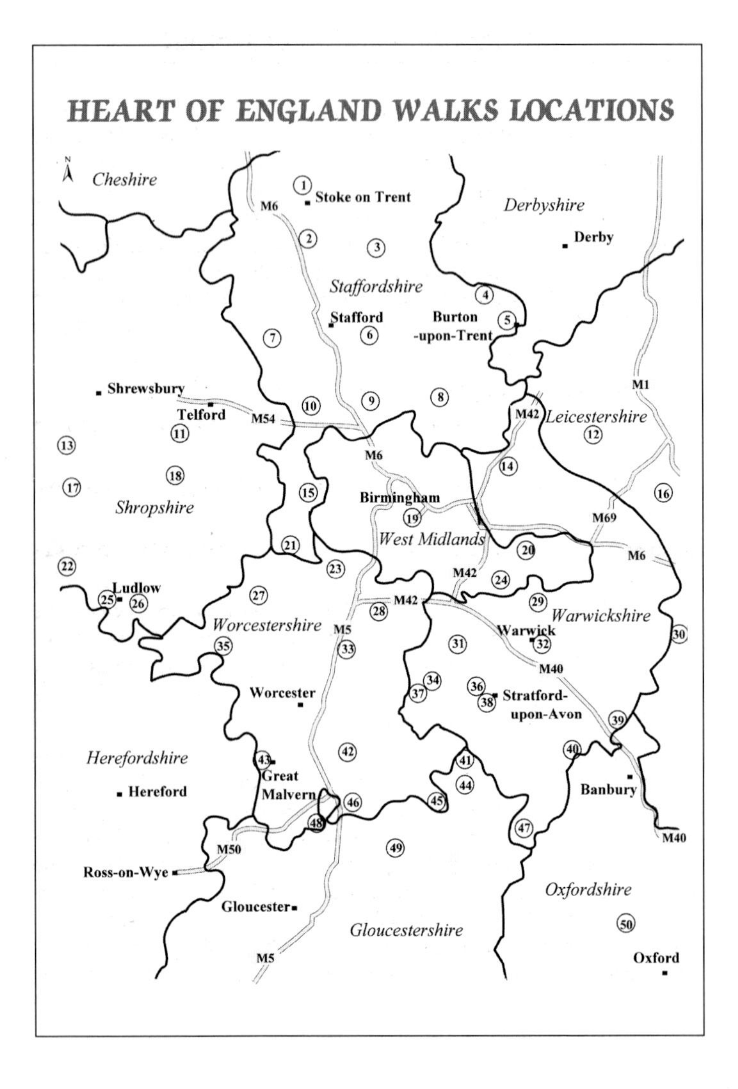
HEART OF ENGLAND WALKS LOCATIONS
N
Cheshire
Stoke on Trent
M6
Derbyshire
Derby
Staffordshire
Stafford
Burton
-upon-Trent
Shrewsbury
Telford
M54
M1
M42
Leicestershire
M6
Birmingham
Shropshire
West Midlands
M69
M6
M42
Ludlow
M42
Worcestershire
M5
Warwickshire
Warwick
M40
Worcester
Stratford-
upon-Avon
Herefordshire
Great
Malvern
Hereford
Banbury
M50
M40
Ross-on-Wye
Oxfordshire
Gloucester
Gloucestershire
M5
Oxford
1
2
3
4
5
6
7
8
9
10
11
12
13
14
15
16
17
18
19
20
21
22
23
24
25
26
27
28
29
30
31
32
33
34
35
36
37
38
39
40
41
42
43
44
45
46
47
48
49
50

Introduction and Background

The sparkle of a country river meandering through a scenic valley, a visit to a typical old English pub in a picturesque village of thatched cottages set amid yellow daffodils in spring, the delight of a colourful narrowboat passing under an ornate canal bridge, a stroll over rolling hills where panoramic views take one's breath away, the vision of a historic castle or large hall set in attractive English countryside. These are a few of the wonderful experiences that can be enjoyed in abundance in the beautiful Heart of England. It is a landscape admired by **William Shakespeare** and the birthplace of many renowned poets and writers including:

A E Houseman, famous for *A Shropshire Lad* (1896);

George Eliot, who made her reputation as a great moral realist with *Adam Bede* (1859);

Izaak Walton, best known for his treatise on fishing, *The Compleat Angler* (1653);

Samuel Johnson, who produced *A Dictionary of the English Language* (1755); and

Michael Drayton, best known for 'Since there's no help, come let us kiss and part' from the sonnet sequence *Idea's Mirror* (1594–1619). His epic *Poly-Olbion* (1598–1622) is a 'chorographic description' of Britain's rivers, mountains and forests, intermixed with folklore (including the story of Lady Godiva).

Whilst there is no precise definition of the area covered by the Heart of England, Meriden in the West Midlands near to Birmingham claims that the medieval cross on its village green marks the very centre of England. For the purpose of this book my Heart of England covers a general area within an approximate radius of 25 miles (40km) from the centre of Birmingham, the second-largest city in England. It embraces the counties of West Midlands, Worcestershire and Warwickshire with parts of Shropshire, Staffordshire, Herefordshire, Gloucestershire and Oxfordshire adding to the wealth of scenic and historic beauty for the walker.

History of the Area

The Heart of England is steeped in history. In Shakespeare's day Birmingham was a market town set in the English countryside amid forests and common land although even then it was noted for a large number of smiths who were making a wide range of iron goods, from door knockers to arms. The Industrial Revolution saw the expansion of trades and crafts and Queen Victoria declared Birmingham a city. It was at the centre of the Industrial Revolution in the 18th century when a large number of canals were built in the area to transport the many products of the industrial midlands and as a freight link for industry throughout the UK. Much of the Heart of England area was involved with the Industrial Revolution. Ironbridge Gorge in Shropshire claims to be its birthplace and has been designated a World Heritage Site. The Staffordshire Potteries are world famous and were a major player on the canals. Kidderminster in Worcestershire built a reputation for manufacturing fine carpets. Today, Birmingham is a modern city whose canals offer a variety of leisure interest for the walker.

A magnificent network of waterways still operates throughout the Heart of England and provides a fascinating insight into this industrial past. James Brindley was the main engineer, building the Staffordshire and Worcestershire Canal in 1772 to transport coal, ironware, glass, pottery and textiles; the Trent and Mersey Canal in 1777 for transporting the china clay of Josiah Wedgwood; and the Coventry Canal (finished in 1790) for carrying coal. Brindley also started the Caldon Canal which was completed by his brother-in-law, Hugh Henshall, in 1778. The Shropshire Union Canal was built by Thomas Telford to transport freight from the West Country to Ellesmere Port, and the Birmingham–Fazeley Canal, engineered by John Smeaton, was completed in 1790 to form a link between Birmingham and the southeast. The 25½ mile (41km) Stratford-upon-Avon Canal links Stratford with the Grand Union Canal at Kingswood Junction. The Oxford Canal, another Brindley engineering feat, meanders through remote countryside linking Oxford with the Grand Union and Coventry canals. Up until the early 1900s these canals were busy commercial operations but with the advent of the motor car they fell into disuse. No longer needed to carry heavy and often dirty industrial loads, the canals have today become a major leisure attraction, offering a fascinating glimpse into history and easy walking access to the many picturesque villages across the Heart of England.

There are many fine old buildings to visit throughout the area where the walker will find castles and history in abundance. In Staffordshire you can visit Shugborough Hall, Lichfield Cathedral and Sudbury Hall, while Ludlow Castle is a Shropshire delight. To the south, Worcestershire boasts Hanbury Hall, Hartlebury Castle, Pershore Abbey, Witley Court and Worcester Cathedral, and at the north edge of the Cotswolds the treasures of Broughton Hall, Hidcote Manor, Snowshill House, Tewkesbury Abbey and Sudeley Castle can be enjoyed. Capability Brown, well known for his picture-style gardens, also designed a number of buildings including Croome Court, Worcestershire (1751–52) with interiors by Robert Adam, and the chapel at Compton Verney, Warwickshire (1772).

No trip into the Heart of England would be complete without a visit to Stratford-upon-Avon, birthplace of William Shakespeare, and the surrounding villages where the history of 'the Bard' unfolds. The following famous Shakespeare doggerel was composed after a drinking bout at the Falcon Inn:

Piping Pebworth, dancing Marston
Haunted Hillborough, hungry Grafton
Dodging Exhall, Papist Wixford
Beggardly Broom and Drunken Bidford

In Shakespeare's day Stratford-upon-Avon had a population of 1500 (London's population was only 200,000 at the time) and was a centre of local government and rural business with one of the finest grammar schools in the whole of the country. Today the population has risen to some 23,000 but the town retains its Shakespeare magic with many historic buildings to be seen – a most attractive tourist town. Visits to Ann Hathaway's Cottage in neighbouring Shottery and to Mary Arden's House at nearby Wilmcote offer two fine walks. The surrounding area of Warwickshire is a county of magnificent castles and large country mansions of national importance – Baddesley Clinton Hall, Charlcote Manor, Chastleton House, Compton Wynyates, Coughton Court, Coventry Cathedral, Farnborough Hall, Kenilworth Castle, Packwood House, Ragley Hall, Warwick Castle and Upton House are all within a relatively short distance.

A number of famous battles have taken place in the Heart of England and these add to the fascinating history of the area. In 1265, at Evesham in Worcestershire, Simon de Montfort was defeated by Lord Edward in the Battle of Evesham. In 1417 Tewkesbury in north Gloucestershire was the scene of one of the bloodiest battles of the Wars of the Roses. The Battle of Bosworth near Market Bosworth in Leicestershire ended the Wars of the Roses in 1485 and the course of English history was changed when King Richard III lost his life to Henry VII, crying 'I live a king: if I die, I die a king.' In 1642, at Edgehill in Warwickshire, the Royalists and Cavaliers fought out a draw in the first major battle of the Civil War, then in the Battle of Worcester in 1651 Cromwell's 'crowning mercy' saw the defeat of Charles II.

Walking in the Heart of England

The area offers a wide range of walking. You can meander by a river on an easy riverside/canal walk or take up the challenge of a more testing hill walk – whatever type of walk you can admire some of the finest scenic views and historic buildings in the UK.

Several attractive rivers meander through the Heart of England, offering a further dimension to a number of the walks in the book. The River Trent flows from Burton-on-Trent in the east following the Trent and Mersey Canal to Stoke-on-Trent. The Manifold River meanders through Ilam on its path north up a beautiful valley on the east of Staffordshire, while the delightful River Churnett carves its way from Rocester to Leek in the north. The River Severn passes through Tewkesbury and on up through Bridgnorth in Shropshire. The River Avon winds through the Vale of Evesham in Worcestershire and continues into Warwickshire, adding to the picturesque scene at Stratford-upon-Avon with its many half-timbered Tudor-style houses and buildings. A number of reservoirs and lakes in the north of the area provide fine scenery and a haven for wildlife. These include Ellesmere, Blithfield, Chasewater, Rudyard, Tittlesworth, Kingsbury Water Park and Staunton Harold.

There are many superb hill walks in the Heart of England. In Shropshire, Wenlock Edge, Long Mynd, Stiperstones and the Clee Hills offer magnificent views over the surrounding countryside and into Wales. Kinver Edge in Staffordshire provides fine countryside views of Shropshire and Worcestershire, and Dovedale on the edge of the Peak

District is a true scenic delight. In Worcestershire, the Malvern Hills rise to 1394ft/425m at the Worcestershire Beacon; at least eight counties can be seen from Bredon Hill on a clear day; the thickly wooded Abberley Hills offer superb hill walking; and the Lickey Hills near Stourbridge provide a weekend retreat for the people of Birmingham, with good views over the busy metropolis. Broadway Hill on the edge of the Cotswolds offers a magnificent view from by its famous folly tower set on the Cotswold escarpment.

The Heart of England is indeed a very fine walking area and there are a number of Walking Ways which you will meet on your travels. The Heart of England Way meanders 100 miles (160km) from Bourton-on-the-Water in Gloucestershire to Cannock Chase in Staffordshire. The Staffordshire Way is a 92 mile (148km) route from Mow Cop to Kinver Edge. The Centenary Way (Warwickshire) circles a 100 mile (160km) route from Kingsbury Water Park in the West Midlands through to Upper Quinton, Warwickshire. The Worcestershire Way is a 47 mile (76km) walk from the Kinver Edge to Malvern in Worcestershire. The Wychavon Way is a 40 mile (64km) walking way from Holt Fleet in Worcestershire to Winchcombe in Gloucestershire. The Arden Way is a 26 mile (42km) circular walk around the former Arden Forest area of Warwickshire starting at Henley-in-Arden. The Heart of England can be said to be the heart of the country's long distance footpaths.

About these Walks

The 50 walks in this book explore this feast of history and beauty. They are designed to allow the walker to visit some of the UK's most picturesque scenes, ancient heritage and attractive villages – some will actually take you past the historic buildings and through the former battlegrounds of England.

The walks vary in length from 1¾ miles (2.8km) to 10 miles (16km) and the walking surface is generally good – all the walks should be within the walking capacity of the average person. In dry weather the paths will be good underfoot and normal outdoor footwear should be adequate for the shorter walks. In wet weather or during winter months there could be some wet stretches of footpath when it is preferable to wear stout, waterproof boots or shoes and to be prepared with wet weather clothing.

There can be few greater pleasures of life than to visit a pub after a pleasant country walk, so the majority of walks either start from an attractive pub or pass a named pub en route. With each walk there is a sketch map of the route which is intended to identify the starting point and which should be adequate to guide you for the walk. Ordnance Survey maps to the scale of 1:25,000 are specially designed for walkers and provide more detailed information. Apart from a detailed walk description, each walk contains preliminary information on the walk distance(s), duration, refreshment availability, how to get to the start, car parking, the type of terrain, and the relevant OS map. Key landmark features from the sketch maps are highlighted in bold type in the walk instructions to aid orientation.

The Country Code

All the routes incorporate public rights of way where there is an onus upon every walker always to follow the Country Code, to look after our precious countryside and to protect the environment for future generations:

Enjoy the countryside and respect its life and work

Guard against all risks of fire

Fasten all gates

Keep your dogs under close control at all times

Keep to public footpaths when walking across farmland

Use gates and stiles to cross fences, hedges and walls

Leave no litter behind you

Safeguard water supplies

Protect wildlife, plants and trees

I wish you happy walking in the beautiful Heart of England.

Roger Noyce

WALK 1 – The Meeting of the Canals at Etruria

An attractive short walk set in the potteries city of Stoke-on-Trent. A delightful towpath walk along two of James Brindley's famous canals will allow you to marvel at the fine engineering and provide an opportunity to visit the Etruria Industrial Museum which is set at the junction of the canals. Initially you will take the towpath of the Trent and Mersey Canal and can then meander through Hanley Park where you will enjoy a lakeside stroll through colourful flowers. The return route is along the towpath of the Caldon Canal.

Distance:	3½ miles (5.6km)
Duration:	Allow 2 hours
Refreshments:	The China Garden (a Toby Inn) sited by the Marina in Etruria (Tel. 01782 260199)
Walk Start:	Stoke-on-Trent is northeast of Junction 15 of the M6 motorway and Etruria is best approached on the A500 road. Follow the signs to the city centre then aim for Festival Park. At the park go left, signposted 'Marina and Entertainment'. The China Garden is on the left (GR 869474)
Car Parking:	The China Garden has a large car park which is open to the public
Terrain:	Easy walking along canal towpaths and on garden paths
OS Map:	Explorer 258 – Stoke-on-Trent and Newcastle-under-Lyme

The famous pottery-making names of Wedgwood, Minton, Copeland, Spode and Coalport still dominate north Staffordshire after some 100/150 years and Stoke-on-Trent is at the very centre. Originally the pottery factories dominated the six towns of Tunstall, Burslem, Hanley, Longton, Fenton and Stoke, and then in 1910 they joined together to become the city of Stoke-on-Trent. Josiah Wedgwood is known as 'the father of the pottery industry' and he built an entire village for his employees and called it Etruria. At the beginning of World War II the Etruria site was badly affected by subsidence and Josiah moved his factory to the village of Barlaston. Sadly, the Etruria area became somewhat derelict but happily an award-winning land reclamation scheme revived the area and it became the venue for the famous National Garden Festival in 1986. Today Etruria is known as Festival Park and is a popular visitor attraction with a wide variety of leisure activities available.

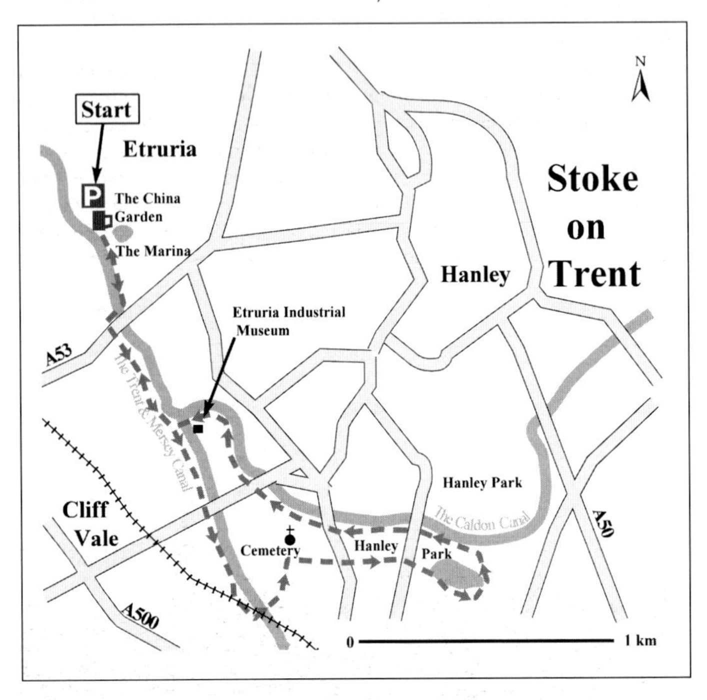

From the **China Garden** car park, proceed over the small drawbridge at the boat entrance to the marina. Follow the towpath of the Trent and Mersey Canal bearing left to pass the **marina** and to reach a canal bridge. Ascend the steps to the left of the bridge, cross over the canal and descend the other side to walk under the bridge and to continue on the towpath which is now on the right side of the canal. In about 400m you reach some lock gates at the junction of the Trent and Mersey and Caldon canals. Continue past the junction on the towpath of the **Trent and Mersey Canal** passing beneath the very low road bridge by Twyford Lock. After some 600m of towpath walking you pass two bottle-shaped brick ovens on your right – these ovens were a common sight in the 19th century but are sadly all that remain of a sizeable pottery complex; opposite you will see the cemetery. In a further 200m you walk past an iron mile post 'Preston Brook 36 miles' and then bear right up from the towpath to go over a footbridge over the railway line and the canal.

Now follow the pavement of the road by iron railings passing by a row of private terraced houses with garages to arrive in Avenue Road and to enter the cemetery via a gate. Take the tarmac path through the **cemetery** bearing generally to the right (northeast) until you reach a road. Now go left and then right crossing the road to enter **Hanley Park** through a large gate. This is a very pleasant garden area with attractive and colourful flower beds and borders. Exit the garden via a further gate crossing the road to enter another area of the park via a large gate.

The meeting of the Caldon and Trent and Mersey Canals

Proceed to the right of an attractive lake then arc left to pass by tennis courts and a crown bowling green. At the back of the bowling green ascend to the park fence and exit the park via a gate to arrive on the towpath of the **Caldon Canal**. Now go left and follow this towpath for about ¾ mile (1.2km). You pass beneath a series of canal bridges as you proceed at the back of factories and houses – the canal is fairly narrow and a meeting of narrowboats is an interesting sight. Soon you arrive at the junction of the two canals where you should walk to the right of the buildings of the **Etruria Industrial Museum** (perhaps spare time to visit) to re-join the towpath of the Trent and Mersey Canal. Here go right and retrace your steps back to the China Garden.

WALK 2 – The Wedgwood Factory Walk

An easy short walk that starts from the attractive village green in the pleasant village of Barlaston. After leaving the village there is a delightful stroll along the towpath of the Trent and Mersey Canal and the opportunity to visit probably the best-known pottery in the UK – here you will be able to experience a little of the amazing industrial history of the Heart of England. After leaving the canal the route allows you to enjoy a scenic lake view on the return to Barlaston.

Distance:	3 miles (4.8km)
Duration:	Allow 2 hours
Refreshments:	The Duke of York pub in the village of Barlaston (Tel. 01782 374221)
Walk Start:	Barlaston is north of Stone and east of Tittensor off the A34 road. Cross the Trent and Mersey Canal and the main railway line to bring you to the centre of Barlaston
Car Parking:	Park with consideration in the village of Barlaston by the side of the road near the village green and library (GR 894384)
Terrain:	Easy walking along towpaths and good footpaths
OS Map:	Explorer 258 – Stoke-on-Trent and Newcastle-under-Lyme

From the large village green, go right and walk in front of the village library (the former school, built in 1680). About 150m beyond the library, cross over the road and go left to take a track set to the right of the modern **Parish Church** of St John the Baptist. The clear track proceeds generally southwest to the left of a hedge and becomes a path over pasture land as it continues to the right of a field hedge. After about 800m go left over a stile to go through the hedge onto a track. Bear left and meander below a railway bridge and then cross the road bridge over the **Trent and Mersey Canal**. Now go left and descend to the canal towpath.

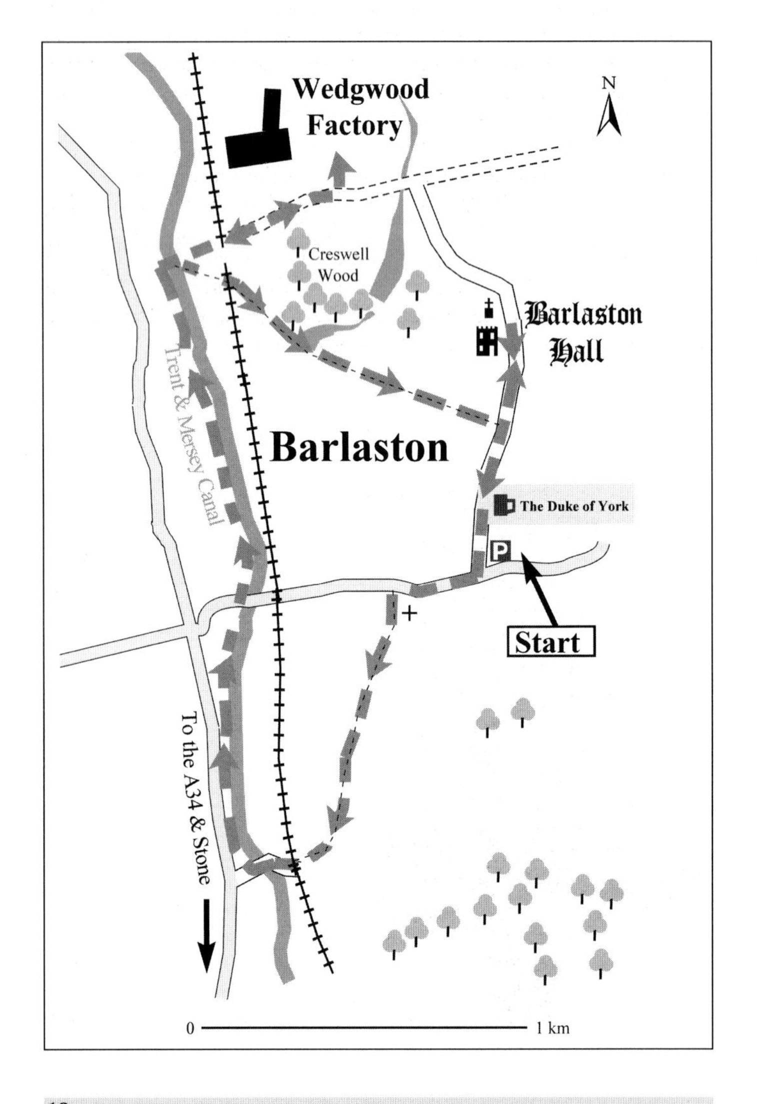
Wedgwood
Factory
N
Creswell
Wood
Barlaston
Hall
Trent & Mersey Canal
Barlaston
The Duke of York
P
Start
To the A34 & Stone
0
1 km

Continue left beneath the bridge for a delightful 1¼ miles (2km) of attractive towpath walking. You are at the rear of attractive residential gardens which pleasingly stretch down to the very towpath and provide floral pleasure during the spring and summer months. After passing beneath the bridge by the Plume and Feather Inn, continue north on the towpath to enjoy a very peaceful scene which is occasionally broken by an inter-city train speeding along the nearby railway line. As you approach the canal bridge no 104, you will soon see the massive Wedgwood factory on the far right bank of the canal, and you can so easily imagine Wedgwood barges drawn by horses and carrying the famous pottery to Birmingham – they must have made quite a sight in the 19th century. Ascend to the road, cross over the Old Road Bridge and walk up the lane to see the **Wedgwood factory**.

Picturesque sign for Barlaston

When Josiah Wedgwood built his new factory at Barlaston (it commenced production in 1940) the rural scene changed very rapidly. The railway line replaced the Trent and Mersey Canal as the main form of transport for materials and products of the famous pottery, and Barlaston was no longer a sleepy village. The Wedgwood Group remains the largest china and earthenware manufacturer in the world and the Barlaston factory is at the centre of the industry with its six 'clean' electric tunnel ovens. The Wedgwood Museum is open to the public.

After your visit to the factory, return to the Old Road Bridge (no 104) over the Trent and Mersey Canal. Just before reaching the bridge, go left through a corner field gate and commence a field walk back to the village of Barlaston. You go through a pair of kissing gates, cross the railway line and then go over stiles to follow the bottom end of a beautiful small **lake near to Creswell Wood**. From the lake ascend the footpath to the next field and to the left ahead you enjoy a superb view of Barlaston Hall. The path leads over stiles to a kissing gate onto Longton Road by a junction with the lane to the Wedgwood complex. To get a closer look at **Barlaston Hall** go left and walk up the lane for a better view.

Barlaston Hall is a fine mid-18th-century building which was the HQ of the Bank of England during World War II. In 1773 a picture of the hall appeared on a dinner service made for the Empress Catherine of Russia. Today it is privately owned and is not open to the public – please respect the privacy of the owners.

Now retrace your steps down Longton Road into the village of Barlaston. You pass some very attractive houses on the right. After passing by the **Duke of York pub** (on your left) you reach the village green.

WALK 3 – Froghall Wharf to Consall Forge

This walk from Froghall Wharf starts with a tranquil towpath stroll along the Caldon Canal up to Consall Forge where you are greeted by a picturesque scene with an attractive weir and probably a steam train on the Churnett Valley Railway. On the return journey you ascend through woodland to the hamlet of Hazlescross and then meander back down towards the Caldon Canal, passing by a wildlife sanctuary. The walk is completed via the canal towpath to return to Froghall Wharf. The wharf is the very end of the canal and is a picture postcard scene.

Distance:	5½ miles (9km)
Duration:	Allow 3 hours
Refreshments:	The Black Lion at Consall (Tel. 01782 550294)
Walk Start:	Froghall is about 11 miles east of Stoke-on-Trent near to the A524 (Stoke-on-Trent to Ashbourne) road. After passing through Kingsley the road proceeds over the River Churnett via the Froghall Bridge. In 200m go left, following the signs to the wharf and its small free car park (GR 028477)
Car Parking:	Free car park at Froghall Wharf
Terrain:	Generally easy walking on the towpath of the Caldon Canal with one steep hill ascent
OS Map:	Explorer 258 – Stoke-on-Trent and Newcastle-under-Lyme; Explorer 259 – Derby, Uttoxeter, Ashbourne and Cheadle

Commence your walk from the attractive picnic site at **Froghall** Wharf, proceeding west along the towpath of the Caldon Canal. This pleasant 2 mile (3.2km) canal walk starts on the left bank towpath crossing over the B5053 canal bridge (no 54) to go around a short tunnel (76m long and with 6ft/1.8m headroom for the narrowboats) and soon you are walking between the **Caldon Canal** and the **River Churnett**. You pass by bridge no 53 – this is Cherry Eye bridge which got its name from the condition of ironstone miners' eyes when emerging from their

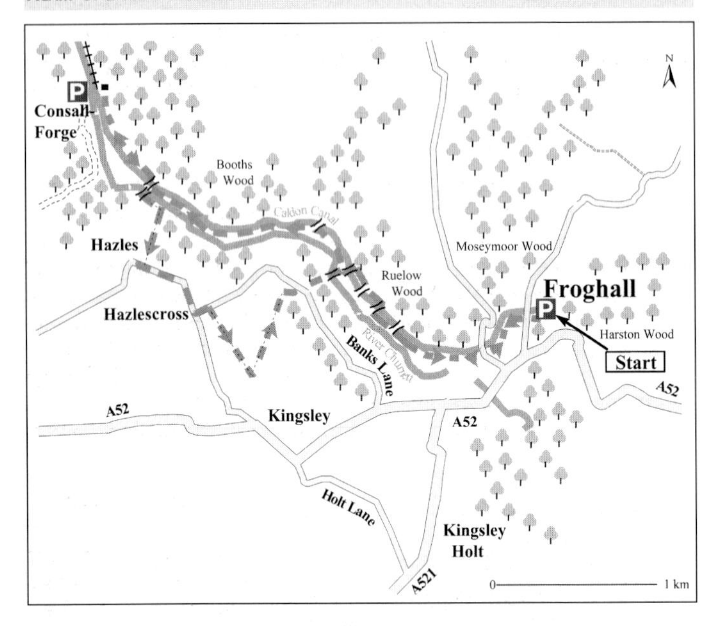

tunnels. Cross over the canal at the next bridge and walk on the right bank towpath going beneath the railway bridge before returning to the left bank at bridge no 49. Once again you will be walking between the canal and the river. Cross over to the right bank by bridge no 48 and follow the towpath past Consall Forge Pottery, the remains of Consall Upper Flint Mills and the new railway station of Consall before arriving by the Black Lion Inn at **Consall Forge**.

Consall Forge is a tiny hamlet which during the Industrial Revolution bustled with a variety of mineral works along the banks of the River Churnett. Today all that remains of the industrial background is a bank of overgrown lime kilns sited near to a car parking area. Consall Forge has become a quiet backwater – a peaceful and beautiful place which is only occasionally ruffled by a passing narrowboat or by a steam train on the Churnett Valley Railway. It is here that the River Churnett and the Caldon Canal split over a fine weir.

From the Black Lion return along the towpath of the Caldon Canal, going past Consall Railway Station. In about 750m you pass the Consall

Forge Pottery once again to reach a bridge over the canal. Go right to cross over the canal and the railway line and to ascend through Hazles Wood – follow the red walk waymarkers of Froghall Wharf Walks. This is a short but steep ascent and you will soon arrive in Hollins Lane near to the hamlet of **Hazles**.

Go left along the lane to the neighbouring hamlet of **Hazlescross**. At the road junction go left into the hamlet, then in about 100m go right through a gate into open countryside. Proceed southeast over two fields and a stile and enter a third field. Look out for a red waymarker in about 60m and here go left (northeast) to continue over fields to a gate into woodland. To the left is a wildlife sanctuary. As you descend the hill steps you pass close to the sanctuary – they serve light refreshments if you wish for a break. Continue by descending the hill through woodland. After crossing a footbridge over the River Churnett, cross the railway line and you arrive back on the towpath of the **Caldon Canal** at bridge no 53.

Go right and take the canal towpath into Froghall. You pass a huge factory complex before arriving at bridge no. 54 – the B5053 goes over the canal here. The attractive Froghall Wharf picnic site is reached after going around the short tunnel again. The wharf marks the very end of the 17 mile (27km) long Caldon Canal. If you fancy a return journey you can travel on the Froghall Passenger Service which runs return boat trips from the wharf to Consall Forge.

The short tunnel near Froghall Wharf

WALK 4 – Tutbury Castle and the River Dove

This walk will take you through the interesting old streets of Tutbury, and there is an opportunity to visit a local glass blowing factory where you can see the craftsmen practising their skills. You will follow the pleasant riverbank of the Dove, passing near to the historic remains of Tutbury Castle which stand proud above the village.

Distance:	2 miles (3.2km)
Duration:	Allow 1½ hours
Refreshments:	The Leopard pub in Monk Street, Tutbury
Walk Start:	Tutbury is about 4 miles (6.5km) northwest of Burton-upon-Trent. The A50 road passes through the town and Duke Street is found by following the road signs to 'Free Car Park (toilets)' (GR 211289)
Car Parking:	Park in Duke Street car park, Tutbury
Terrain:	Easy walking on good footpaths
OS Map:	Explorer 245 – The National Forest, Burton upon Trent

From the Duke Street car park go left and walk down Duke Street. Opposite is Silk Mill Lane where the premises of Georgian Crystal may be visited, and Tutbury Glass can be found at the bottom of Burton Street on the corner of Ludgate Street. To continue your walk go up the attractive olde worlde High Street where you pass by several antique shops and Ye Olde Dog and Partridge Inn.

Tutbury, originally known as Totta's Burgh, was a fortified place in the Saxon Kingdom of Mercia and was recorded in Domesday Book as being one of only three burghs in the country – and the only one to have a market. The town has attracted a number of skilled craftsmen and women and today you can see the local artists at work in the towncentre premises. An artist, a clock maker, jewellery makers, wrought iron workers and glass engravers provide a fascinating display of skills for the visitor to enjoy. Tutbury glass is probably the most famous and at their premises you can see glass being blown into shape.

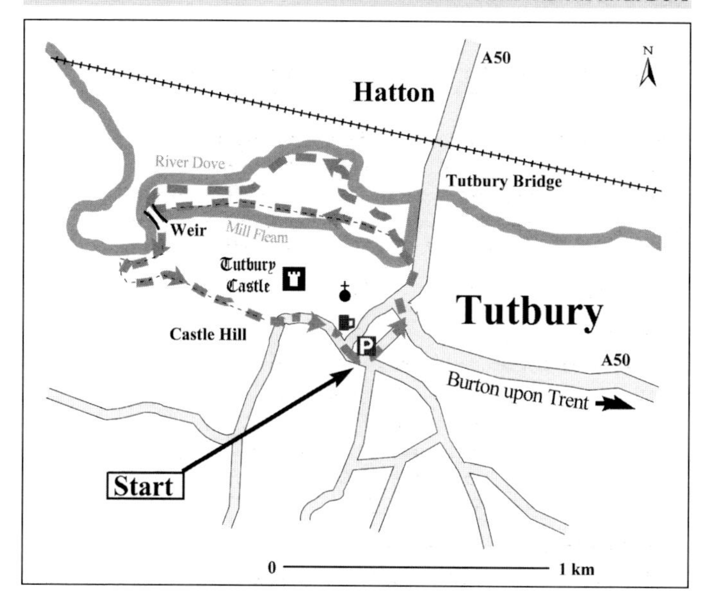

At the end of the High Street bear left, then right to walk down Bridge Street and you soon reach a road island where the **A50** road passes through Tutbury.

Just after passing by the road island go left to enter a landscaped picnic area with car park. This was the site of Tutbury Mill, which once produced cotton and later converted locally mined gypsum into plaster – it closed in 1968 and has been converted into a leisure and recreation area for Tutbury's residents. Proceed through the park to a stile by the side of the cricket pitch and you arrive in open countryside. The official waymarked path is straight ahead to the right of a waterplant-covered stream called **Mill Fleam**. Mill Fleam is in fact the feeder stream to the old cornmill situated on the other side of Tutbury. Alternatively you can follow the clear, well-worn path along the bank of the attractive **River Dove**. This meandering Dove-side walk is a delightful alternative, which has been walked by local people for many years, and up to your left you can see the remains of the impressive Tutbury Castle.

Set upon the hill overlooking Tutbury are the ruins of Tutbury Castle – its most famous royal visitor was Mary Queen of Scots who was imprisoned in the castle on three occasions while she was held at the mercy of Elizabeth I.

Main gates of Tutbury Castle

You soon reach the weir which lets water into Mill Fleam. Cross over the footbridge at the **weir** and walk along the riverbank for a short distance to go over a stile. In 50m bear left and then left again along a footpath which now leads you generally towards the castle and back towards the village of Tutbury. After going over a couple of stiles and a footbridge you ascend **Castle Hill** and here you can decide whether to visit the ancient castle. Continue ahead to go through a small gate and between buildings to reach Park Lane. Go left and descend the pavement into Tutbury and to the Duke Street car park.

WALK 5 – The Brewery Capital of the UK

This short easy walk offers the delights of natural waterside countryside together with an opportunity to visit the historic parts of Burton-upon-Trent – the home of brewing in the UK. At Burton-upon-Trent you will walk through the Washlands which are attractive low-lying lands adjacent to the River Trent. They have been recognised for their value to leisure and wildlife, comprising a delightful mix of open meadows, wetlands, woods and waterways.

Distance:	3 miles (4.8km)
Duration:	Allow 2 hours
Refreshments:	The Boathouse at Stapenhill (GR 253219)
Walk Start:	Burton-upon-Trent is east of Staffordshire. The Trent Washlands are south of the town and are best approached on the A444 road. Start at the road island near St Peter's Church
Car Parking:	Use the public car park about 200m along Stapenhill Road beyond St Peter's Church (GR 255223) – you can join the walk by descending to the riverbank
Terrain:	Easy walking on good footpaths
OS Map:	Explorer 245 – The National Forest, Burton upon Trent

Burton-upon-Trent has, since the Middle Ages, been known as the home of British brewing and still produces its beer in individual barrels. William Bass began brewing in Burton in 1777. Michael Bass, who became Lord Burton in the 19th century, gave the town many of its finest buildings, including the town hall and the churches of St Paul and St Modwen. In 1998 Bass acquired the brewery of Carlsberg-Tetley to create a site of 830 acres, brewing 5.5 million barrels of beer per year and becoming the largest brewery site in the UK. The Marston's Brewery has been brewing in Burton for over 150 years and visitors are invited to see their working cooperage and to enjoy a pint of famous Pedigree Bitter. Burton Bridge Brewery was established in 1982 to meet the needs

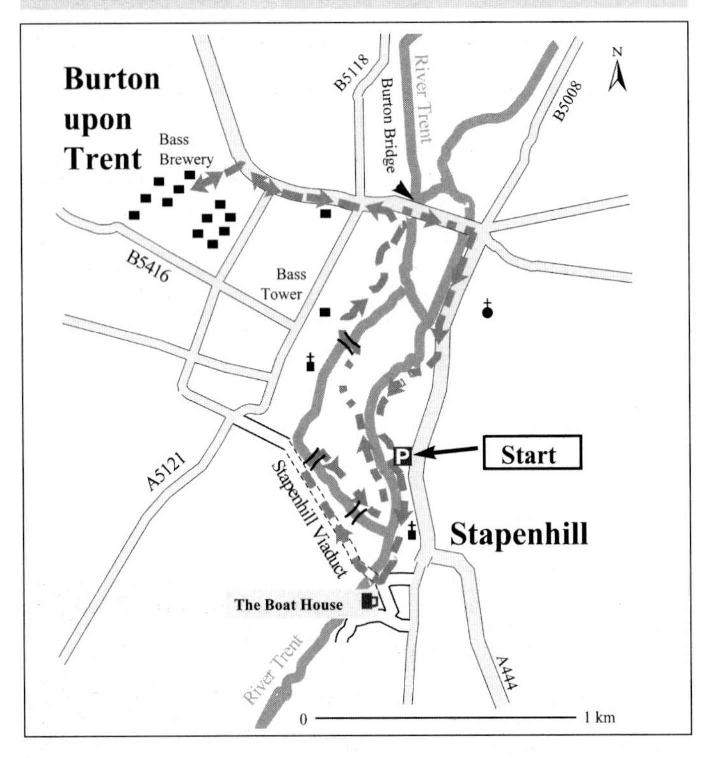

of the real ale enthusiast. The River Trent passes through the town and is crossed by three bridges.

From the car park in Stapenhill Road proceed south past **St Peter's Church** and beneath St Peter's Bridge (built in 1985) to enter the beautiful Stapenhill Pleasure Gardens – a true picture of colourful flower beds. Continue on the path and you all too soon arrive by the superb Ferry Bridge (opened in 1889 when there was a toll of ½d per person). Proceed over **Stapenhill Viaduct** (a raised walkway which was a gift from the Baron of Burton in 1889). This delightful 500m walk offers pleasant views over the surrounding Trent Washlands. Just before the end of the viaduct, go right and descend onto a tarmac path and cross a footbridge over the Silverway stream. Go right and walk by the side of the Silverway to reach the River Trent. Continue on the tarmac path now by the side of the Trent and then go left to walk to the right of rugby football pitches to reach the Cherry Orchard play and picnic area.

Proceed past the Cherry Orchard to reach the Trent side near to St Modwen's Church (on the other side of the Trent). Bear right and cross over the Andresey Bridge. To your left is **St Modwen's Church** and the garden of remembrance. To your right is the huge **Bass Brewery Tower**. You may wish to visit these, then continue by bearing right and follow the lane to **Burton Bridge** (opened in 1964) – spare time to walk down to the weir for it is most attractive. Ascend the path to the A50 road and go left along the pavement to enter Bridge Street and to see the Burton Bridge Inn.

Weir on the River Trent, with Burton Tower behind

Burton Bridge Inn has parts dating from the 17th century and is the second oldest remaining pub in Burton. The Burton Bridge Brewery was established in 1982 to cater for an increasing demand for real ale and has won many awards for excellence. The inn is a small friendly brewery tap room that sells five or six Burton Bridge beers – a chance to taste a locally brewed real ale.

Continue past the inn into Horniglow Street where you find the huge **Bass Brewery** complex.

The Bass Museum site covers some 6 acres having been set up in 1977 to celebrate the 200th anniversary of Bass in the town. The fascinating museum includes a superb collection of historic vehicles and there is a scaled 2000 building and working model railway of Burton in 1921.

Now retrace your steps past the Burton Bridge Inn walking over Burton Bridge on its wide footpath where there is a good overhead view of the weir. At the bridge end, go right and take the pavement of the A444 road. You pass the blue **boathouse** of Burton-upon-Trent Sea Cadet Corps and Burton Leander Rowing Club before bearing right to walk along a path by the side of the River Trent once more. The tarmac path meanders along the bank of the river passing Stapenhill Hollows and you soon reach the Stapenhill car park up on the left.

WALK 6 – Shugborough Hall and the Canals

A very fine waterside walk and an opportunity to visit the famous Shugborough Hall. The walk starts from a picturesque lane in the village of Great Haywood, crossing over the Trent and Mersey Canal and the River Trent packhorse bridge. The route proceeds to the front of the superb Shugborough Hall and after crossing back over the River Trent you will join the towpath of the Staffordshire and Worcestershire Canal. This meets the Trent and Mersey Canal for the return to Great Haywood.

Distance:	4 miles (6.4km)
Duration:	Allow 2½ hours
Refreshments:	The Clifford Arms pub in Great Haywood offers a warm welcome to walkers
Walk Start:	Great Haywood is east of Stafford and just west of the A51 (Lichfield to Hixon) road. The Clifford Arms is in Main Road, Great Haywood (GR 997226)
Car Parking:	Walkers who become patrons at the Clifford Arms may park in its large car park by arrangement with the licensee (Tel. 01889 881321)
Terrain:	Easy walking on canal towpaths and on good footpaths
OS Map:	Explorer 244 – Cannock Chase and Chasewater, Stafford

From the car park of the **Clifford Arms**, go right then right again to take a short but picturesque lane beneath a railway bridge. Proceed over bridge no 73 of the Trent and Mersey Canal and over the superb 16th-century packhorse bridge (Essex Bridge) across the River Trent.

The lovely old Essex Bridge is just 4ft (1.2m) wide with 14 beautiful arches and offers a great photo opportunity at twin forks of the River Trent beneath the bridge. Because the bridge was not wide enough to carry a horse and carriage, the Anson family of

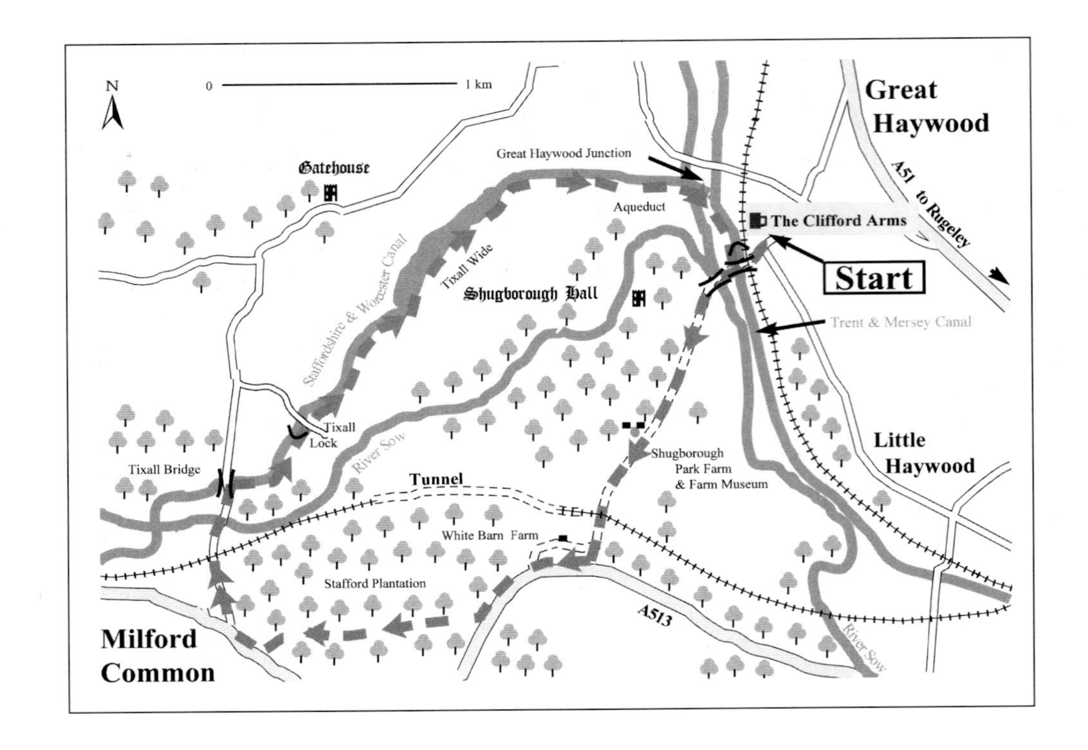

N
0
1 km
Great Haywood
A51 to Rugeley
Gatehouse
Great Haywood Junction
Aqueduct
The Clifford Arms
Start
Tixall Wide
Staffordshire & Worcester Canal
Shugborough Hall
Trent & Mersey Canal
Tixall Lock
River Sow
Tixall Bridge
Shugborough Park Farm & Farm Museum
Little Haywood
Tunnel
White Barn Farm
Stafford Plantation
A513
River Sow
Milford Common

Shugborough Hall had a wider bridge built about 100m downstream to avoid having to walk some 300m to church each Sunday!

Proceed past the tradesman's entrance to Shugborough Hall and take a fenced tarmac track past the hall itself – there is a fine view of the magnificent building of Shugborough Hall to the right.

Shugborough Hall was built in 1693 and later enlarged by Thomas Anson. The wings were added in about 1748 and then in 1794 the eight-columned portice completed a superb façade. The inside of this National Trust property is richly decorated with Rococo plasterwork and there are fine collections of 18th-century ceramics, silverware, paintings and French furniture.

Continue by going to the left of **Shugborough Farm** and its pleasant small lake, taking the farm drive and crossing the bridge over the railway line. Where the drive arcs right, proceed ahead on a footpath that leads to the A513 road. Now go right and take the pavement of the road past the drive/entrance to Shugborough Farm Museum where the Arch of Hadrian will catch the eye.

This copy of Hadrian's Arch in Athens is on the site of the original village of Shugborough and was built for Thomas Anson in 1761 to celebrate Anson's circumnavigation of the world in 1740–44. The arch contains the busts of Admiral Lord Anson and his wife.

About 200m beyond the entrance to the farm museum, go right again and ascend an attractive tree and fern lined footpath through **Stafford Plantation** and over a short hill. At the top of the hill take the path past a raised reservoir (enclosed in railings) and commence a descent on a clear wide track/path to the left of a stone wall. This leads back down to the A513 road. Now go right along the pavement of the road, passing by a pair of fine Milford Lodges (1800) and the main entrance to Shugborough Hall. Just past the entrance gates, go right and descend the road to Tixall. Proceed over a railway bridge and then over the River Sow. At the **Tixall Bridge** (bridge no 106 of the Staffordshire and Worcester Canal) descend to the towpath and go right (east) to take the right-hand bank of the canal. The towpath passes by **Tixall Lock** and beneath Oldhill Bridge (bridge no 107) to reach the **Tixall Wide**.

Tixall Wide is a 300m stretch of the canal which was deliberately widened to form a sort of lake to the former Tixall Hall. Up to the left the massive 16th-century gatehouse can still be seen. It is one of the largest in the UK, being three stories in height, and is richly decorated with Roman, Ionic and Corinthian columns. There are four impressive, tall turrets which give the impression of an old folly. The Tixall Wide is often used for mooring narrowboats, and fishermen, patiently waiting for a catch, form part of a pleasing scene as you walk past.

Shugborough Hall (National Trust)

Continue along the towpath beneath a swivel bridge (bridge no 108) and then past the clutter of colourful narrowboats congregating near the repair facilities at the Great Haywood Junction. Proceed under the elegant sweeping arch bridge at **Great Haywood Junction** – a bridge made famous by the photography of canal historian Eric de Maré. Bear right now to follow the towpath of the Trent and Mersey Canal. Just after passing Haywood Lock leave the towpath at bridge no 73. Pass beneath the bridge and ascend to go through a hand-gate onto a lane. Now go right and retrace your steps over the canal going beneath the railway bridge and up the short picturesque lane to return to Great Haywood. The Clifford Arms is on the left.

Situated near the entrance to the Trent and Mersey Canal, the black and white frontage of the Clifford Arms is an inviting vision in the summer when it is adorned with hanging flower baskets. The original old Coaching Inn Hotel building was destroyed by fire in the 1930s. It was rebuilt, in part using Italian POW labour, and the superb parquet floor in the bar/lounge is a particular feature – it was built by the Italians and has been lovingly restored by the present owners.

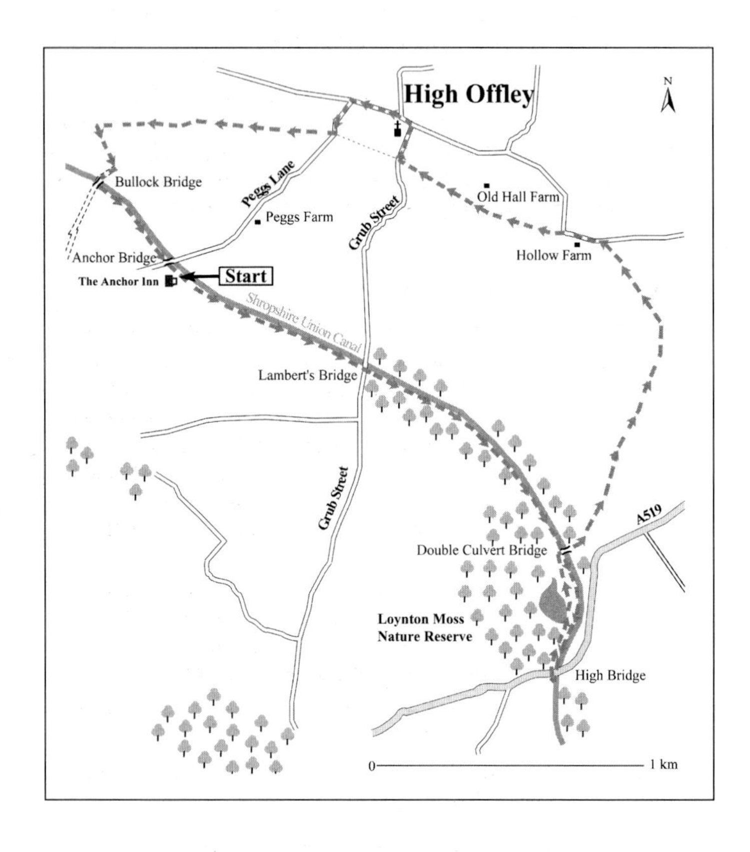
High Offley
N
Bullock Bridge
Peggs Lane
Peggs Farm
Grub Street
Old Hall Farm
Hollow Farm
Anchor Bridge
The Anchor Inn
Start
Shropshire Union Canal
Lambert's Bridge
Grub Street
A519
Double Culvert Bridge
Loynton Moss
Nature Reserve
High Bridge
0
1 km

WALK 7 – The Telegraph Bridge at High Offley

A walk along the towpath of the Shropshire Union Canal is always a pleasure and the famous telegraph pole bridge is a sight to behold in this delightful part of Staffordshire. This easy walk starts from the historic Anchor Inn by the side of the attractive canal. The route leads below the pleasant village of High Offley, offering fine views, and meanders down to the Telford Masterpiece Canal to visit the amazing bridge no 39 – here you will see a telegraph pole set within the bridge structure. The walk concludes with a gentle canalside walk back to the inn.

Distance:	4 miles (6.4km)
Duration:	Allow 2½ hours
Refreshments:	The Anchor Inn on the Shropshire Union Canal
Walk Start:	High Offley is west of Stoke-on-Trent and is reached on the A519 road from Eccleshall – the village lies south of Eccleshall. The Anchor Inn is on the canal bank in Peggs Lane; to reach it drive past the church in High Offley and take the next left turn – the inn is on the left just after crossing the canal bridge (GR 775256)
Car Parking:	The Anchor Inn has a large car park which may be used by walkers who patronise the inn. Alternatively park with consideration near the church in High Offley (GR 784261)
Terrain:	Easy walking on fairly level ground and along the canal towpath
OS Map:	Explorer 243 – Market Drayton, Loggerheads and Eccleshall

High Offley is a remote and peaceful village set in attractive Staffordshire farming countryside. The word Offley comes from the medieval word Offleie – an extensive tract of land. This tract of land is bisected by the Shropshire Union Canal which is overlooked by the 700-year-old village church imperiously set on a hilltop in the village.

From the the Anchor Inn descend to the towpath of the **Shropshire Union Canal**. Go right and meander the canal towpath heading southeast. You pass beneath **Lambert's Bridge** (bridge no 41), Double Culvert Bridge (no 40) and then High Bridge (no 39) – the famous telegraph bridge. Pause here to admire a superb view of this unique bridge – it is the sole survivor of the many telegraph lines which once existed on the canal banks throughout the country. Now bear right and ascend from the canal to reach the A519 road. Cross over the road and proceed up the path opposite into **Loynton Moss Nature Reserve**.

Loynton Moss is mentioned in Domesday Book, having been formed in the Ice Age about 10,000 years ago. Today within the pleasant woodland look out for Common Reed, Greater Reedmace and the Lesser Celandine. You may also be lucky enough to spot a Sedge Warbler or a Speckled Wood Butterfly.

Meander through the lovely woodland for some 450m and then exit onto a track. Go right over **Double Culvert Bridge** (bridge no 40) and proceed through the copse on the far bank. Exit the copse via its gate and take the clear path going northeast over several fields. You pass to the left of buildings and the waymarked path passes to the right of a sycamore tree. After walking this field path for about 800m you reach a rather dilapidated car repair area. Bear left through this and then walk to the left of a field hedge going generally northwest. In about 300m you go over a hedge stile onto a lane. Here, go left past **Hollow Farm**.

At the first bend in the road, bear left through a gate and go over a stile into pastureland. Take the clear waymarked path as it continues in a general northwest direction. Proceed to the left of the hedge. You go through a hedge gap and over a couple of stiles before reaching a road called Grub Street. Go right up Grub Street to arrive in the village of **High Offley**. At the road junction bear left through the village and in about 250m go left again down Peggs Lane. Take the quiet Peggs Lane for just over 100m, then go right over a stile and follow the path going west. As you keep to the left of the field hedge, go through a field corner gate and then over a footbridge crossing a further field to its hedge. Now go left again and in 150m go right onto a wide track. Take this track which leads to **Bullock Bridge** (bridge no 43) on the Shropshire Union Canal.

Cross over the bridge and descend to the canal towpath. Now take the towpath going southeast and after passing beneath **Anchor Bridge** (bridge no 42) you soon arrive back at the Anchor Inn.

Set on the banks of the Shropshire Union Canal, the Anchor Inn was built in 1827 to provide refreshments for canal workers and bargees when the canal was first built by Thomas Telford. It has retained its simple alehouse character and still holds its original furnishings which include settles and tables – a veritable treasure which now appears in books of famous inns. The current landlord has occupied the inn for 27 years and it has been in his family for some 100 years.

The amazing 'telegraph pole' bridge

WALK 8 – Lichfield Cathedral Walk

A pleasant walk through attractive Staffordshire countryside with the opportunity to visit and meander through the beautiful city of Lichfield with its wonderful three-spired medieval cathedral.

Distance:	4½ miles (7.2km)
Duration:	Allow 3 hours
Refreshments:	There are numerous eating/drinking establishments in the city of Lichfield
Walk Start:	The car park in Pool Walk
Car Parking:	Pay and display car park in Pool Walk near to Minster Pool (GR 116097)
Terrain:	Easy walking in the city and over good footpaths in the countryside
OS Map:	Explorer Map 232 – Nuneaton and Tamworth, Lichfield and Atherstone

From the car park aim for the Minster Pool bearing right into Dam Street to join the Heart of England Way. Now go left over the bridge and the magnificent cathedral is ahead of you. Bear left, walking along the side of the **cathedral** to reach its superb frontage – spare time to visit while your boots are nice and clean.

Lichfield Cathedral is a renowned medieval cathedral unique for its three wonderful spires – they have earned it the nickname 'Ladies of the Vale'. A sandstone masterpiece, it has a memorable west front displaying a mass of superb statues. Cathedral Close has sweeping secluded lawns and there are charming medieval black and white cottages (where the professional choristers live) to admire in Vicars Close.

When you are ready, leave the cathedral via The Close, going right along Bird Street then left into Shaw Lane where you descend to reach the recreation area. Proceed on the clearly waymarked path going through a car park and along the back of a row of houses with football pitches and then a **golf course** to the left.

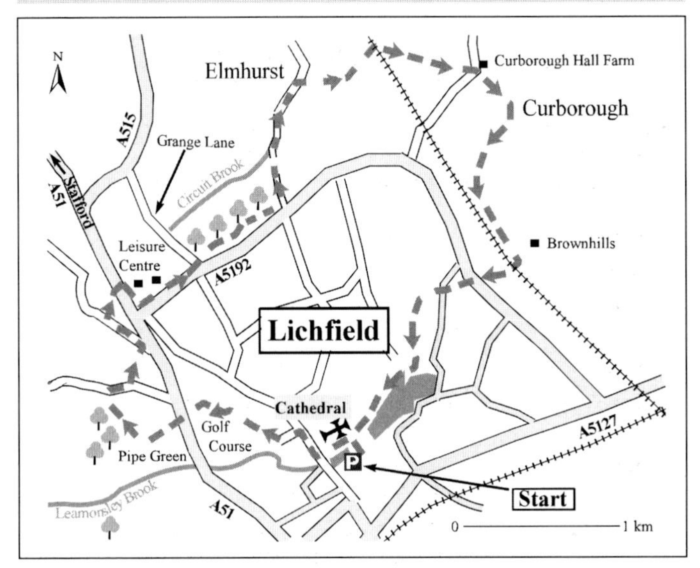

Continue, going over two stiles to reach the A51 (Stafford–Lichfield) road. Cross the busy road with care and go over the stile opposite, then take a field path to cross a footbridge. Now bear generally right aiming for a stile in the far corner of the next field. Go over the stile and follow a hedged track (with an ancient moat to the right) until you reach Abnalls Lane by Maple Hayes Hall entrance (a dyslexia school) on the left. Go right along the lane for about 120m, then go left over a stile at a 'Public Footpath' sign and walk to the right of a hedge of cultivated field. Cross to the left side of the hedge before going over a further stile into Cross in Hand Lane.

Go left and ascend the narrow lane for 250m then, just after passing the entrance drive to Lyncroft Cottage, go right and take a pleasant hedged path which proceeds north to arrive at the A51 (Stafford to Lichfield) road. Cross over the A51 and go right along a footpath near the roadside – it is set in trees above the road level. Walk to a road junction with traffic lights and here go left along the pavement of Eastern Avenue (the A5192). Proceed past the entrance to Friars Grange **Leisure Centre** and you soon reach **Grange Lane**. Cross over the lane and veer left up some steps and onto a path in a (mainly) conifer plantation. Continue northeast along the clear path which meanders through the trees with glimpses of Lichfield to the right and pastureland to the left. In about 500m the path reaches the open with Dimbles Lane on the other side of Eastern Avenue and you see some steps up from the Avenue. Here, go left onto a driveway and continue northeast to cross over the entrance drive to a car parking area.

Proceed on the clear path opposite (known as the Dimbles) initially descending between trees to go over **Circuit Brook** and then ascending among ivy-clad trees to reach a green lane (Fox Lane) which leads into the pleasant Hamlet of **Elmhurst**. At the green lane end, go right onto a farm track which arcs left to pass a finger post as you join the Darwin Way going northeast. Take this clear track past Apsley House and then where the track (now a concrete lane) bends sharp right proceed ahead over a field towards a railway line. Go over the stile onto the railway and cross the line (the trains speed through so take care). Proceed over the stile opposite and continue in a southeast direction over several fields – you go through a kissing gate, by the side of an electric pylon and through a farm gate to arrive on a lane by **Curborough Hall Farm** complex.

Walk past a small antique centre and go to the right of the farm buildings, a number of which now house an art and craft industry. At the sign to Field House, walk to the right of the drive hedge, veering left as it bends to go over a footbridge and stile in the top left-hand corner of the field. Here you leave the Darwin Way and go right (southwest) to walk by the side of a small babbling brook to reach and go over a field corner stile so that you can continue on your path line, the three spires of Lichfield Cathedral now prominent ahead on the skyline. The path arcs left to go over a stile then runs generally parallel with the railway line to your right. Continue over several stiles with a farm lane to your left until you reach a bridge over the railway. Cross over the bridge and proceed over Chadswell Heights road into a dead-end residential lane. Immediately after the first house, go left and follow a tarmac footpath behind houses and you soon emerge into Spring Road. Now walk ahead and then go right at the road corner along a further footpath which leads into Netherstowe Lane. Here go right to cross over Eastern

Avenue and follow the footpath opposite into Verdi Court and then to Netherstowe Road.

Cross over the road and take Handel Walk to the right opposite. This path leads to a footpath/cycleway in pleasant parkland. Bear left and follow this path initially to the left of football pitches and later past allotments until you reach St Chad's Road. You will see the impressive St Chad's Church to your left as you cross the road and ascend steps onto a walkway where there is a fine view of Stowe Pool. Bear right and take the poolside path with fishermen, ducks, coots, moorhens and seagulls adding to a most pleasing view.

At the end of the pool you cross over Bishop's Walk to arrive in Reeve Lane which leads you back into Dam Street near the cathedral. If you go left over the bridge you will enjoy a delightful view of Minster Pool on your return to the car park.

Lichfield is a very attractive provincial city with ornate and decorative facades to its shops and inns – Daniel Defoe declared Lichfield City to be a 'A fine, neat, well built city'. It is a leisure town of the Georgian period, where lovely gardens and pools (situated near to the magnificent Cathedral) help to make the important early ecclesiastical centre a city of true grace. Dr Samuel Johnson was born here and his cream coloured house can be seen on the corner of Breadmarket Street.

The impressive west front of Lichfield Cathedral

WALK 9 – A Cannock Chase Experience

A delightful stroll onto Cannock Chase – this former home of the Pagets (Marquises of Anglesey) was once a huge deer park for royalty and the nobles of England but is now very attractive woodland and heathland which is open for the public. The walk will take you through Beaudesert Old Park in the southern part of the Chase.

Distance:	5 miles (8km)
Duration:	Allow 3 hours
Refreshments:	The Park Gate Inn, immediately opposite Castle Ring car park, welcomes walkers
Walk Start:	Castle Ring is above the village of Cannock Wood, at the bottom of Cannock Chase. From the A5 road above Brownhills take the B5011 road going north. Continue north at Chase Terrace and take the straight road that leads up into the village of Cannock Wood
Car Parking:	Free car park at Castle Ring (GR 035127)
Terrain:	Easy walking mainly on forestry footpaths
OS Map:	Explorer 244 – Cannock Chase and Chasewater

From the car park take the **Heart of England Way** path at its rear and proceed through the trees in a northwest direction to reach a clear broad track going generally north into Cannock Chase. Bear right onto the track and proceed north for just under 1 mile (1.5km) – the track leads through **Beaudesert Old Park**. At the fork in the track/path, bear left and cross over a small stream by an attractive forest pool. The track now continues generally north towards the Rugeley Road.

Do not walk onto the Rugeley Road, but go right just before reaching it and continue on a path within the trees as it meanders in a northeast direction for about 300m – you then go left to cross over **Rugeley Road** at a junction of four roads (this is at **Wandon**). Here, bear left onto a marked track, still following the Heart of England Way. The track becomes Marquis Drive and you go through two gates before

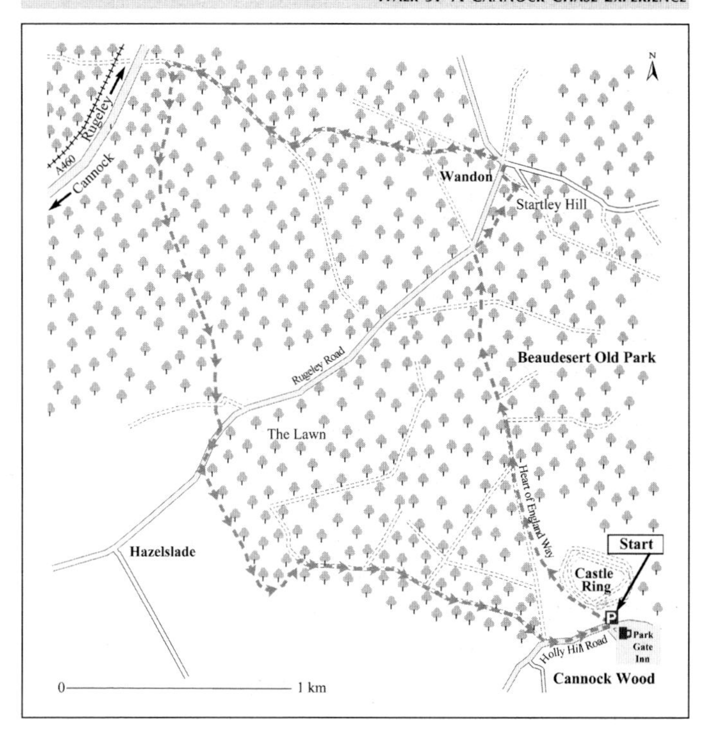

veering left to go past Seven Springs. Here, the delightful track bears right and descends a very attractive valley with a stream and Lower Cliff on the right – if you are lucky you may see kingfishers by the stream as you descend towards the A460 road.

About 100m before reaching te A460, go sharp left past a forestry barrier and ascend a track that bears generally south into the trees. Bear right at a fork in the track and then proceed ahead at a junction of paths/tracks. You ascend between superb conifers before the track levels and then you reach a crossroads of tracks and the perimeter of a golf course. Continue over the golf course but do keep to the path. You soon reach a further junction of tracks. Here proceed ahead and descend a track to reach the **Rugeley Road**.

Track going north into Cannock Chase

Go left along the Rugeley Road for about 200m. When opposite the car park entrance to the golf club, go left by a forestry barrier and take a conifer-lined track that after a while arcs left in a southeast direction and passes by a former colliery pit – now a pool. Ascend the track as it continues through the forest to a crossroads of tracks. Continue ahead and before long you arrive at the **Holly Hill Road** on the edge of Cannock Wood. Go left along the quiet road and in about 300m you reach the Park Gate Inn with Castle Ring car park on your left.

WALK 10 – Medieval Brewood and the Shropshire Canal

Brewood (pronounced 'Brood') is a fascinating medieval village which has a fine range of historic buildings for you to explore. It is the finale to this delightful figure-of-eight walk which takes you along the towpath of Thomas Telford's Shropshire Union Canal and into the surrounding countryside where you will have pleasing views and can enjoy the flora of the area and a wide variety of birdlife.

Distance:	3 miles (4.8km)
Duration:	Allow 2 hours
Refreshments:	The Admiral Rodney Inn, Dean Street, Brewood
Walk Start:	Brewood is northwest of Wolverhampton, just west of Coven off the A449 (Wolverhampton to Stafford) road
Car Parking:	The Admiral Rodney in Dean Street (GR 884085) has a car park for the use of customers. Alternatively you can park with consideration by the roadside in the village of Brewood
Terrain:	Easy walking on good footpaths
OS Map:	Explorer 242 – Telford, Ironbridge and The Wrekin

From the car park at the Admiral Rodney, go right and ascend Dean Street. In about 100m, when opposite to the churchyard of St Mary and St Chad, cross over the road and enter a signed footpath between buildings to join the Staffordshire Way. Take the path going generally south, initially between buildings and then over two fields, until you reach a stile by **Dean's Hall Bridge** (over the Shropshire Union Canal). Go over the stile and go right to take the lane over the bridge and continue along the Staffordshire Way as it proceeds southwest towards **Woolley Farm**. Take the hedged lane passing to the left of the farm. The lane veers left at a lane junction (Hyde Farm is to the right) and you

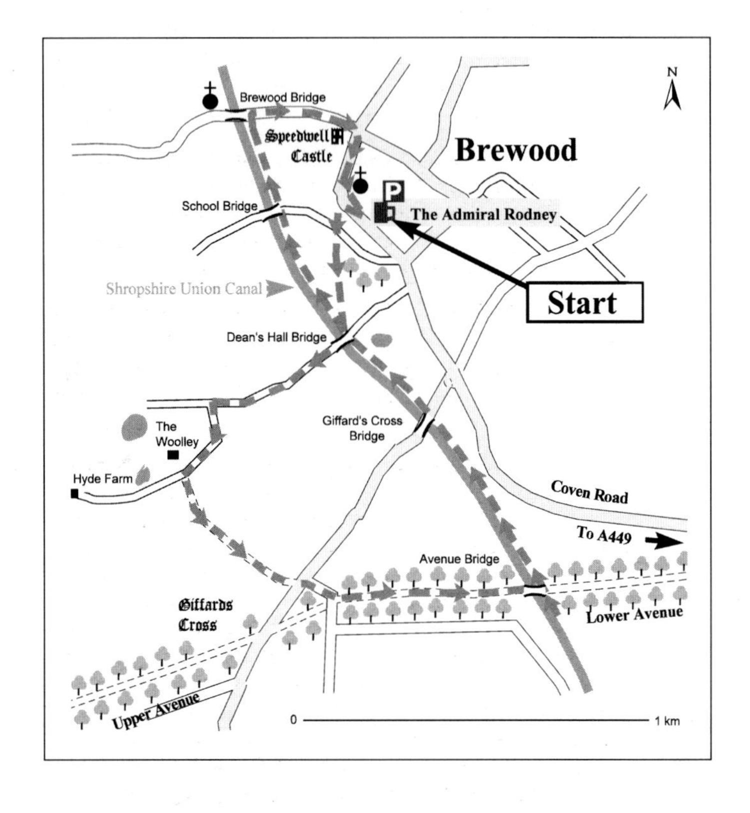
N
Brewood Bridge
Speedwell Castle
Brewood
School Bridge
The Admiral Rodney
Shropshire Union Canal
Start
Dean's Hall Bridge
The Woolley
Giffard's Cross Bridge
Hyde Farm
Coven Road
To A449
Avenue Bridge
Giffards Cross
Lower Avenue
Upper Avenue
0
1 km

will proceed through a farm gate as the lane arcs southeast with a fine view of Brewood to your left. In about 450m you reach a road. Cross over the road and walk up Park Lane opposite.

At the first lane corner, go left onto the lovely tree-lined Lower Avenue. In about 500m you reach Avenue Bridge over the canal and should descend to the towpath. Walk a little way southeast then turn back on yourself to enjoy the fine reflection of the unusual bridge balustrade in the canal. Now go northwest beneath **Avenue Bridge** and follow the towpath of the Shropshire Union Canal beneath **Giffard's Cross Bridge**.

If you choose to go right you reach Chillington Hall, the home of the Giffard family since the 12th century. The hall (built in the 18th century) and the gardens, landscaped by 'Capability Brown' in about 1730, are open to the public during the summer. The park is open all year and is a favourite place with local walkers.

Soon you pass beneath **Dean's Hall Bridge** and a fine view of Brewood will appear to your right. This pleasant stretch of canal walking continues beneath **School Bridge** until you arrive at **Brewood Bridge**. Here leave the towpath, going right through a white gate to arrive in Brewood opposite the Bridge Inn.

Brewood is a delightful medieval village – a tranquil place, steeped in history and full of treasures. Mentioned in Domesday Book and situated in Brewood Forest, the village was visited by several early kings for royal hunting. It has been a centre of Catholicism since the 16th century and was closely associated with the escape of Charles II after the Battle of Worcester in 1651. Much of its Georgian character has been retained and the area was designated an Outstanding Conservation Area in 1969. The oldest building (1350) is Old Smithy Cottages, but there are many 18th-century buildings, for example St Dominic's School (1798), the former workhouse, and Speedwell Castle (1740). Speedwell Castle is an ornate Gothic house reputedly built by a local apothecary using his winnings on a horse called Speedwell. The old pump and horse trough in the attractive Market Place mark the site of the parish pump and here there is a signpost revealing Brewood's significant success in Staffordshire's Best Kept Village competition. The Church of St Mary and St Chad contains the altar tombs of the Catholic Giffard family of nearby Chillington Hall.

Speedwell Castle in the village of Brewood

Now go right to follow the pavement of High Green into the centre of **Brewood**, initially along Bargate Street and then bearing right into Market Place. As you enter Church Road, walk through the churchyard of St Mary and St Chad. Here you will find the grave of Colonel William Careless, a soldier who, after the battle of Worcester in 1651, hid King Charles II in the Royal Oak at nearby Boscobel House. Leave the churchyard via a gate to arrive back in Dean Street. Now go left past yet more lovely old 18th-century buildings until you arrive back at the Admiral Rodney.

WALK 11 – Magnificent Ironbridge and Benthall Hall

A pleasant walk in and around the historic town of Ironbridge, passing by four museums (a visitors' passport can be of value), a craft centre, a National Trust house and an impressive power station. Combined with a stroll above the River Severn this is a walk of varied interest.

Distance:	6 miles (9.6km)
Duration:	Allow 3 hours
Refreshments:	The Boat Inn, Coalport, and numerous eating houses in Ironbridge and Broseley
Walk Start:	Ironbridge is 6½ miles (10.5km) south of Telford. Leave Telford on the A442 road going south then bear right onto the A4169 and onto the B4373 Bridgnorth road. Cross the bridge over the River Severn and bear right for the car park
Car Parking:	Pay and display car park near the Iron Bridge Tollhouse (GR 672033)
Terrain:	Generally easy walking. One hill climb. Paths generally good underfoot but some could be muddy in wet weather
OS Map:	Explorer 242 – Telford, Ironbridge and The Wrekin

Leave the rear of the car park (Tollhouse Museum) by walking the cycle path along the right bank of the **River Severn**. The good path leads through Ladywood, passing through a couple of gates and going beneath a road bridge to continue east. You will see the top of the bridge over the River Severn to the left and soon pass by houses in the village of Coalford. Continue on the road into Jackfield where you will have the opportunity of visiting the impressive **Jackfield Tile Museum**.

Proceed along the road to the left of the museum and past the fine old village church. Continue along the quiet road until you reach the

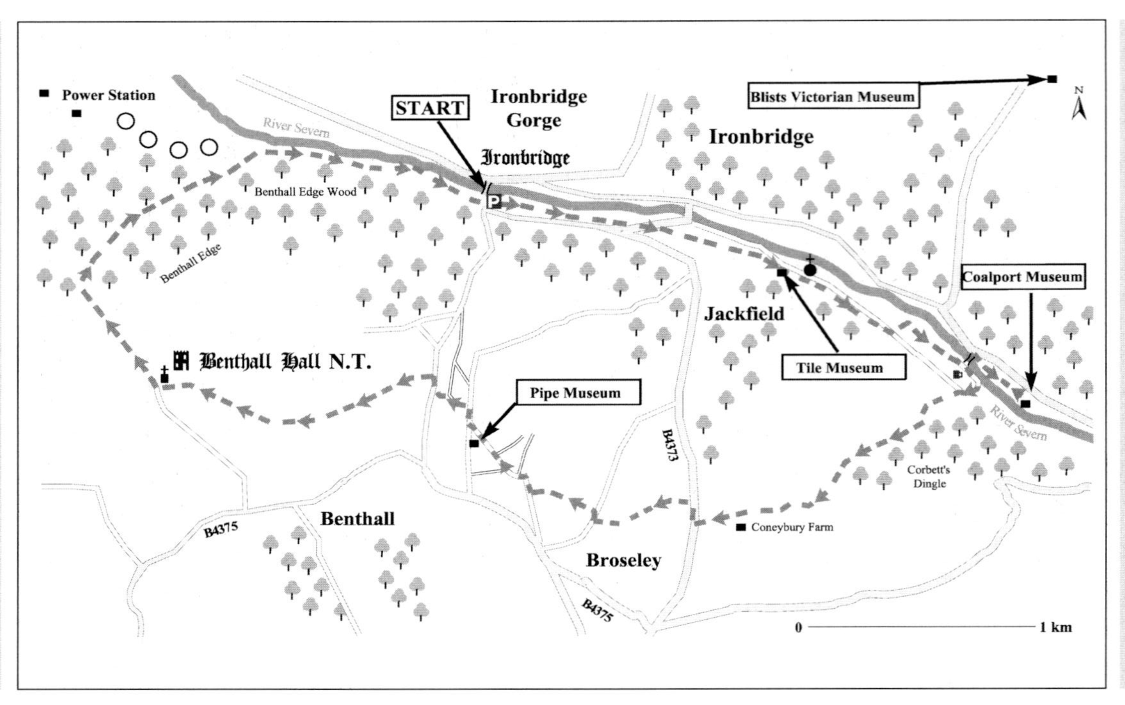
Power Station
River Severn
START
Ironbridge Gorge
Ironbridge
Ironbridge
Blists Victorian Museum
N
Benthall Edge Wood
Benthall Edge
Jackfield
Coalport Museum
Benthall Hall N.T.
Tile Museum
Pipe Museum
River Severn
B4373
Corbett's Dingle
Benthall
B4375
Coneybury Farm
Broseley
B4375
0
1 km

Maw Craft Centre. Take the path to the left of the centre and you emerge in Ferry Road and pass several cottages and the Boat Inn. Here you can cross the bridge to visit the Tar Tunnel and the **Coalport Museum**. The lane arcs sharply right back on itself and where it reaches the dismantled railway line walk beneath the former railway bridge going west. In about 120m the lane bears right and you proceed through the entrance gates to Orchard House and take a track which leads into **Corbett's Dingle**. The track becomes a clear path as it ascends near the right edge of the attractive dingle through trees and with some areas of rock to the right.

Exit the dingle via a gate and continue on a gated track going generally southwest. To your left is **Coneybury Farm** and you take its farm drive to arrive at the B4373 (Bridgenorth–Ironbridge) road.

Go right at the B4373 and in 60m cross the road and go left through a kissing gate and take a clear path which arcs left to proceed up the edge of woodland. After leaving the trees there is a view to the left of Broseley Church and soon you pass through a gateway onto a good track which leads up to Dart Lane in **Broseley**.

Go right for 90m then cross over Dark Lane to continue up Brick Meadow Road. Walk to the end of the road bearing right until you arrive in Duke Street. Go right along Duke Street and continue past Queen Street. You pass by the entrance to the Broseley **Pipe Museum** adjoining which is Quaker Graveyard, where Abraham Derby is buried. At the end of Duke Street, go right along King Street to pass by Holly House – this was the place where in 1782 a constituted court for the settling of small debts met for the first time. Next is Powell's Shop, apparently covered with amazing local tiles. In 25m go left to descend Legges Hill where you pass by Legges Hill School. Proceed down the hill bearing right into Simpsons Lane and in about 50m look for the entrance to Ding Dong Steps on the left. Descend this attractive path at the back of domestic gardens and soon you arrive at Bridge Road. Go right along Bridge Road for about 40m then cross over and ascend a steep tarmac footpath between houses. The tarmac soon becomes grass/soil and eventually you reach a stile by farm buildings.

Go over the stile then walk to the right of the farm building and go over a second stile onto a clear farm track. Take this track going

The historic Iron Bridge, Shropshire

generally southwest for some 450m – a fine stretch of easy walking over a couple of stiles and with a pleasant Shropshire view to enjoy. Bear right to go beneath electric pylon wires to a further stile. Here, bear right again towards the building of **Benthall Hall** along a fine avenue of horse-chestnut trees. You pass in front of the hall and its ha ha where you can enjoy a fine view of the NT property. Continue past the church of St Bartholomew to go through a hand-gate onto the hall drive. Spare time to visit the delightful church and the historic hall.

Continue the walk from the hand-gate by crossing the drive and taking the drive to Benthall Hall Farm. Go to the left of the farm and take a clear farm track to reach a gate into **Benthall Edge Wood**. Go through the gate, following the Shropshire Way waymarkers. Initially the path veers left and then at a junction of paths go sharp right on a woodland track. Within a few yards/metres bear slightly right to take a clear footpath that runs parallel with the track and then gently pulls away from it. Continue on the footpath which descends to the right of a wire fence and soon you enjoy a fine view of the Cooling Towers of Ironbridge Power Station with the Wrekin (1336ft/407m) clearly visible behind them. The path descends further into woodland with an abundance of wild flowers lining the path. As you progress generally northeast you will see the towers to your left apparently getting larger all the time. When you are level with the fourth tower find the path to the left to get an impressive, clear view – they are huge. Return to the main path and continue to a junction of paths near the River Severn.

Bear right and follow the finger post signed 'Ironbridge'. Take this attractive clear woodland path for the next 600m. You will have glimpses of the River Severn to the left below and the hills and houses above the Ironbridge–Buildwas road. The path descends to join a gravel/tarmac lane which you take and soon you emerge from the trees by the amazing **Ironbridge** and your parked car.

WALK 12 – Bosworth Battlefield Walk

An easy walk around the Bosworth battlefield area – an opportunity to visit one of the most famous battlefields in English history.

Distance:	1¾ miles (2.8km)
Duration:	Allow 2 hours
Refreshments:	Battlefields Visitor Centre or perhaps the Hercules Inn at Sutton Cheney
Walk Start:	The Market Bosworth Battlefield is about 7½ miles (12km) north of Hinckley. From Hinckley take the A447 road towards Ibstock. Go left at the turn to Sutton Cheney then follow the signs to the battlefield. Go past the main entrance and left at the T-junction to the car park
Car Parking:	Shenton Station car park (£1 contribution)
Terrain:	Easy walking along the canal towpath and on very good footpaths
OS Map:	Explorer 234 – Rutland Water and Stamford

Leave Shenton Station and walk down the very quiet lane heading southwest. After about ½ mile/1km you cross bridge no 35 over the **Ashby Canal** and go immediately left through a hand-gate to join the canal towpath.

Follow the towpath where yellow iris plants are a treat in spring and colourful narrowboats help create an idyllic scene. Leave the towpath at the next canal bridge via a wooden hand-gate by an old metal-sided railway bridge and go left to cross over the wooden planked bridge to a gravel footpath just inside Ambion Wood. Now stroll the pleasant tree-lined path.

In about 500m bear right and climb away from the main footpath. This path bends to reach a hand-gate near a sign '**Ambion Wood**'. Proceed northeast inside the wood edge. You pass signs 'The Marsh' and 'Richard's Left Flank' which reveal the layout of the Bosworth battlefield.

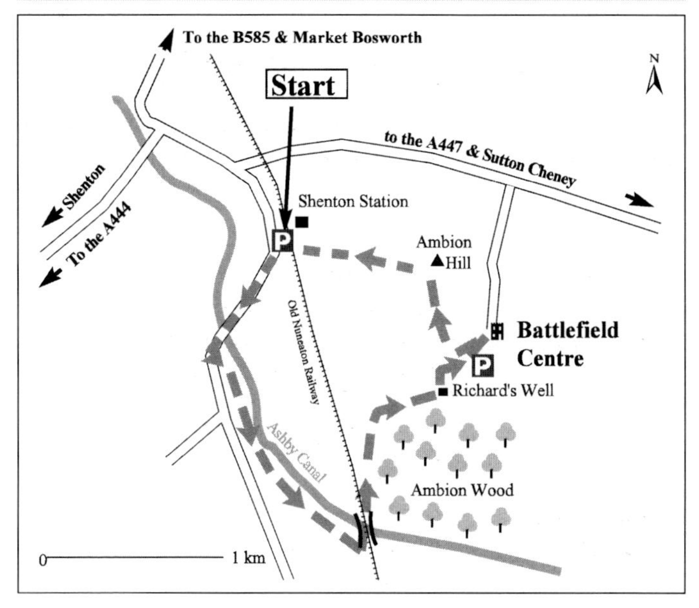

At the wood end you reach **Richard's Well**, which displays a Latin inscription which translates to:

> *Richard III, King of England slaked his thirst with water drawn from this well, when engaged in most bitter and furious battle with Henry, Earl of Richmond and before being deprived of both his life and his sceptre on the morning of 22 August AD 1485.*

Proceed through the metal hand-gate at the back of the well and walk up to the **Battlefield Centre**. As you leave the centre follow the sign to Shenton Station aiming for the top right-hand corner at the end of the parking area.

You can now take a good path which meanders down the slope to reach Shenton Station. You pass by a series of battlefield signs which illustrate the extent of the battleground in 1485 The signs are 'King Richard's Vanguard', 'Richard's Command Position', 'Northumberland's Force', 'Origin of Yorkist Charge', 'The Stanley Forces' and 'The Charge'.

Richard's Well has a Latin inscription

As you continue downhill proceed through a wooden hand-gate by the final sign, 'Henry Tudor's Front Line', and then through a further gate where a 'Heart of the Battle' sign and a standard flies proudly. Cross the bed of the old Nuneaton Railway station cutting (now restored as the Bosworth Light Railway) and **Shenton Station** and its car park lie ahead.

WALK 13 – The Stiperstones Walk

A fine panoramic walk along the Stiperstones, a chain of jagged tors formed 480 years ago – the remnants of a quartzite ridge There is a shorter walk for those who prefer a taste of hill walking and a longer version for the hill walking enthusiast.

Distance:	Short walk 4½ miles (7.2km), longer walk 7 miles (11.2km)
Duration:	Short walk 2½ hours, longer walk 4 hours
Refreshments:	The Stiperstones Inn, Stiperstones
Walk Start:	Leave Church Stretton on the A49 Ludlow–Shrewsbury road by Burway Road bearing right up Carding Mill Valley to the road junction at Bridges (past the Horseshoes Inn). Go left then right, signed 'The Bog', along a narrow road over cattlegrids
Car Parking :	Stiperstones car park (GR 369976)
Terrain:	Hilly. Generally good paths which are rocky and difficult underfoot by Manstone Rock and Devil's Chair
OS Map:	Explorer 216 – Welshpool and Montgomery

From the car park return to the road and go right. Follow the quiet road, enjoying the pleasant view to the left and ahead, until you reach a road junction where go right again. In about 200m (after passing the Shropshire Way Path signs) go right over a stile and take a waymarked path going right over a stile and proceeding up a clear green track to the right of a fence/stone wall. Continue over a couple of fields and stiles now going generally northeast. Three rock formations are prominent on the Stiperstones range to your right – right to left they are Cranberry Rock, Manstone Rock and the Devil's Chair.

At the path junction go left (northwest), still with the low wall to your left. In about 300m go left through a field gate and cross diagonally to go over a further stile onto a main track.

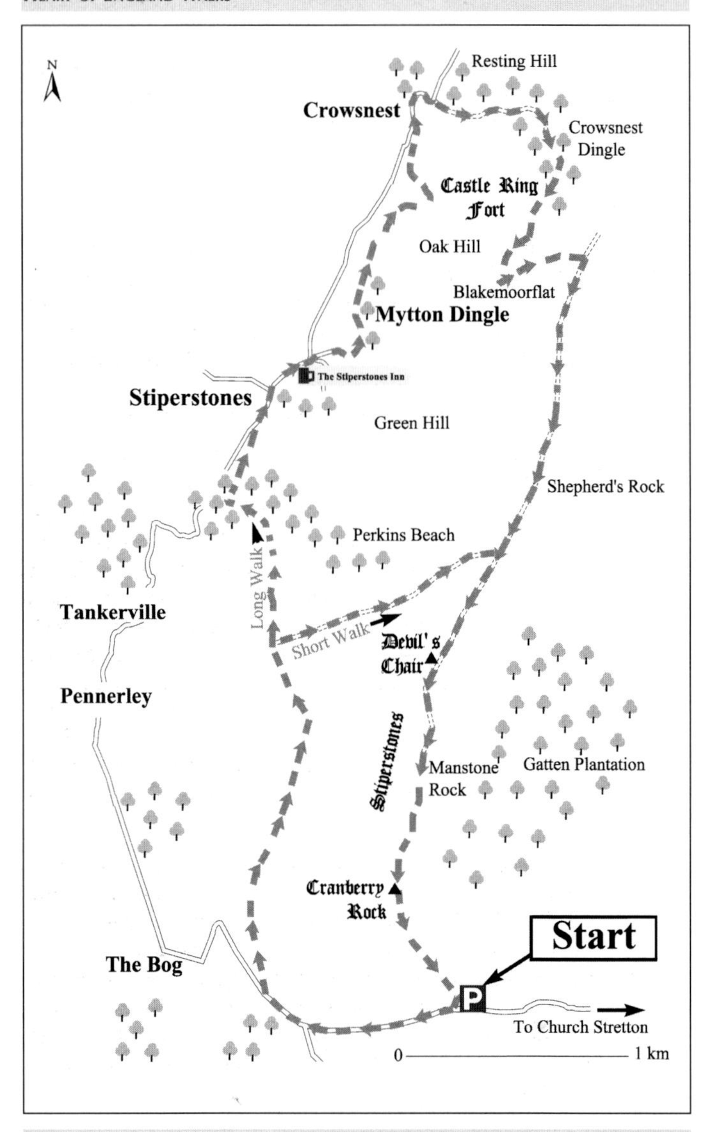
N
Resting Hill
Crowsnest
Crowsnest Dingle
Castle Ring Fort
Oak Hill
Blakemoorflat
Mytton Dingle
The Stiperstones Inn
Stiperstones
Green Hill
Shepherd's Rock
Perkins Beach
Long Walk
Tankerville
Short Walk
Devil's Chair
Pennerley
Stiperstones
Manstone Rock
Gatten Plantation
Cranberry Rock
Start
The Bog
To Church Stretton
0
1 km

Short Walk
Go right up the main track going northeast. There are fine views all around as you ascend gently to the top of the Stiperstones ridge and reach a wide rocky path at the top. Here, go right and walk towards Devil's Chair.

Long Walk
Cross over the main track and descend the path opposite. The fern path meanders initially north and then arcs left descending sharply to a stile into pasture land. Go over the stile for a super view of Stiperstones village with the Welsh mountains beyond. Now descend the field bearing right at its bottom to walk by the field hedge towards **Stiperstones village** with Oak Hill prominent to the right. As you near the first house go over a stile and descend left to reach a road.

Go right and take the quiet road through the village. You pass by a school and the **Stiperstones Inn** on your right. Immediately past a new BT telephone box, go right through Mytton Vale bus depot. Veer right to go over a stile that leads to a hillside footpath. Take this footpath going generally north for the next ½ mile/1.2km. Initially it is like a balcony walk with a fine open view to your left and then it meanders around **Oak Hill**. On the right is a fern bank while a farmer's barbed-wire fence to the left will keep you on the path. After a few twists and turns and undulations you go through a hand-gate and in front of a white cottage. The green path arcs left and then right onto a stone track. Descend this track over a stile to reach the road once again into a lane past Crows Nest Farm. Take this valley road going through the hamlet of **Crowsnest** with Resting Hill high to your left and Oak Hill high to your right.

The lane veers right and soon you commence a footpath ascent. In about 600m you reach the top of the valley and ahead is a super view of Corndon Hill while the village of Stiperstones nestles below. Go sharp left on the clear track and ascend by a wall/fence until you reach a main track. Go right and ascend this mainly green wide track that leads along the crest of the Stiperstones range. As you progress along the heather-clad ridge the view of Devil's Chair becomes ever prominent but there is a fine panoramic view all around – a superb stretch of hill walking.

The beautiful track over the Stiperstones range

Some ¾ mile/1.4km after joining the track you meet another track (the short walk) ascending from the right.

Short and Long Walks

Take the very clear ridge track towards Devil's Chair. It becomes a rocky track and you will need to take care but a fine panoramic view is a good reward for your effort. The rocks were apparently prised from the tors in severe frosts during the glacial period.

Proceed up to **Devil's Chair**.

Legend says that when the Devil intended to fill the valley between the Stiperstones and the Long Mynd with boulders, the rocky outcrops were formed when he rose from his chair and his apron strings broke.

The fine walking continues as you proceed along the rocky ridge track past **Manstone Rock** (the highest point on the Stiperstones at 1760ft/536m) and **Cranberry Rock** for yet more wonderful views. The track now arcs gently left becoming an easy-to-walk green track as you descend to a stile and the car park – all the time with a fine panoramic view ahead.

WALK 14 – Kingsbury Water Park Stroll

A short but very pleasant easy stroll around the delightful Kingsbury Water Park where there are many birds to see.

Distance:	3½ miles (5.6km)
Duration:	Allow 2 to 2½ hours
Refreshments:	Good selection of pubs and eating houses in Kingsbury
Walk Start:	Kingsbury is 5½ miles (9km) north of Coleshill. Leave the M42 at junction 9 on the A4097 going northeast. Before reaching the road island in Kingsbury go left into Bodymoor Heath Lane and follow the signs to the Visitor Centre
Car Parking:	Park in the pay and display Visitor Centre car park (GR 205960)
Terrain:	Easy walking on good level footpaths
OS Map:	Explorer 232 – Nuneaton and Tamworth

From the visitor centre walk to the end of the parking area and then go left (north) on a wide stone footpath. In about 700m you reach a junction of paths with the noise of the busy M42 motorway to your left. Now go right and continue along the easy Heart of England Way (a clear bridleway path). You pass by **Kingsbury** Pool and the Far Leys complex. The bridleway arcs gently to the right and in about 650m you arrive at a long raised footbridge. Go left and proceed onto the footbridge/footpath but just before you reach the bridge over the River Tame, go right on a clear path with the river on your left and **Hemlingford Water** on your right.

Where the path divides, keep to the left path (the right one merely follows the bank of Hemlingford Water) and in about 200m you reach a cycleway lane. Now go left along the lane to cross over Hemlington Bridge. Just before the lane sign 'Kingsbury Road', go left over a stile into riverside pastureland and take the clear path to the left of the road hedge. As you near the field end go over the stile to the right onto the pavement of Kingsbury's A51 Coventry road.

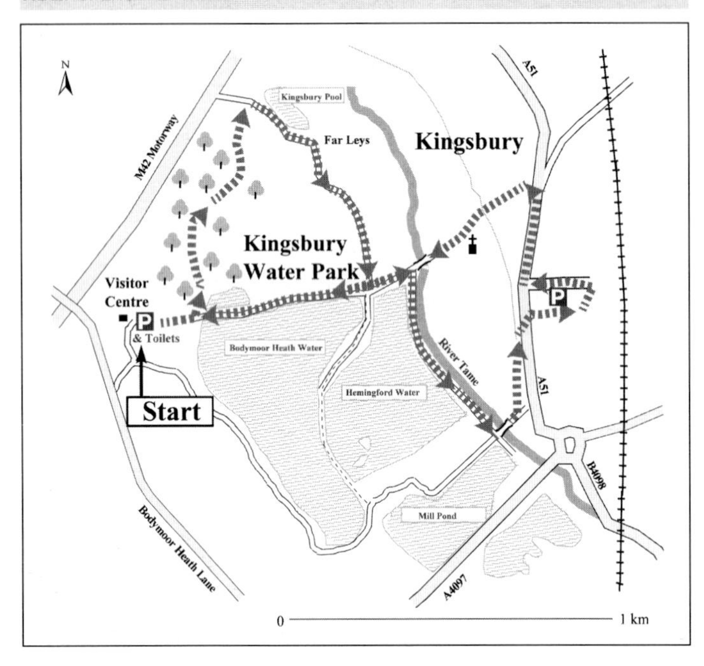

Go left and when you reach Church Lane, cross over the **A51** with care and enter the common land opposite on a path which proceeds ahead to the south of the gardens of houses. In about 200m go left to ascend Wright Close and to reach Pear Tree Avenue. Now go left and follow the Avenue to reach the A51 road.

Cross over the **A51** road (take care going over this busy road), then proceed right. In about 120m go left to walk by the side of the churchyard as you proceed towards the River Tame. Bear right and descend the steps to reach the footbridge into **Kingsbury Water Park**. Cross the footbridge over the River Tame and take the long raised footpath. You soon reach a narrow stretch of land to the left but continue ahead going generally west, past the car park, until you arrive back at the Kingsbury Park **Visitor Centre**.

View of Lichfield Cathedral over the Minster Pool (Walk 8)

Footbridge and stone footpath on the way up the Long Mynd (Walk 17)

WALK 15 – Bratch Locks and the Staffordshire and Worcestershire Canal

This easy walk starts from the famous Bratch Locks at Wombourne and then follows the Staffordshire and Worcestershire Canal into typical attractive Staffordshire countryside and the village of Trysull. Further pleasant country walking leads back to the canal and finally to the Bratch Locks where you can while away many a fascinating hour watching colourful narrowboats negotiate the amazing locks.

Distance:	3½ miles (5.6km)
Duration:	Allow 2 hours
Refreshments:	The Plough Inn, Trysull
Walk Start:	The Bratch Locks are west of Wolverhampton just off the A449 (Kidderminster to Wolverhampton) road. At the road island with the A463 road drive towards Wombourne – Bratch Locks are in just over ¾ mile/1.2km
Car Parking:	Park near Bratch Locks – there is a small car park by the picnic area at Bratch Bridge, Wombourne (GR 868937)
Terrain:	Easy walking along the canal towpath and on good footpaths
OS Map:	Explorer 219 – Wolverhampton and Dudley

From the car park, proceed left over **Bratch Bridge** (bridge no 47) and left again, descending to follow the towpath on the right bank of the Staffordshire and Worcestershire Canal.

The Staffordshire and Worcestershire Canal, which stretches from the River Severn at Stourport-on-Severn to cross over the River Trent at Great Haywood junction in Staffordshire, is a marvellous feat of James Brindley engineering and today is a treasured canal in the hearts of canal enthusiasts. In 1978 the whole canal was declared a Conservation Area to preserve its many features of historic interest.

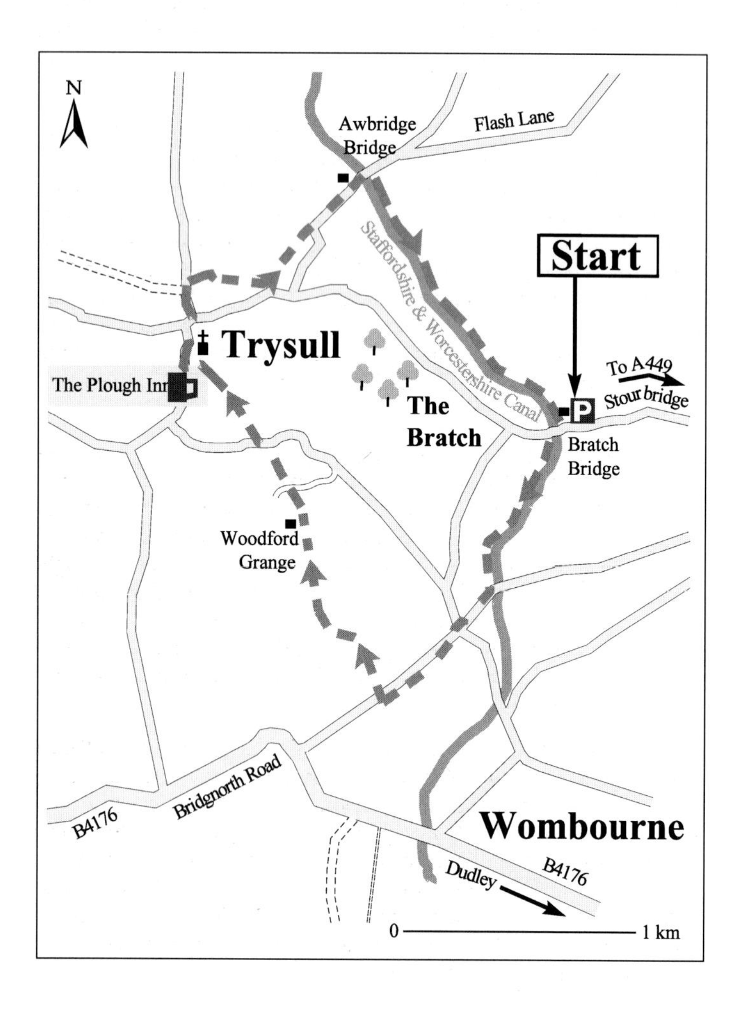
N
Awbridge
Bridge
Flash Lane
Staffordshire & Worcestershire Canal
Start
Trysull
The Plough Inn
To A449
Stourbridge
The
Bratch
Bratch
Bridge
Woodford
Grange
B4176
Bridgnorth Road
Wombourne
Dudley
B4176
0
1 km

As you proceed along the towpath, Bratch Common is on the right and you will be greeted by an abundance of wild flowers in the wetlands which were once a small lake. Continue past Bumble Hole Lock and exit the canal by a narrow path at the next bridge (bridge no 43) to arrive in Poolhouse Road.

Ascend the pavement past the massive Ferro factory on the right and at the top of the hill bear left to take the quiet and safe footpath inside the road hedge of the Meadlands residential estate. In about 400m go right through a hedge gap, cross over the Bridgnorth Road and then enter a waymarked disused road which is protected from vehicle access by two very large boulders. Go through the side gate and take the tarmac road which becomes a track as it arcs left. Proceed over the field stile and aim for a second stile by a farm gate ahead. Now continue the walking line which runs parallel with electric pylons to the right and aim to the right of **Woodford Grange** Farm which you will see ahead.

Pass to the right of the farm buildings and their array of vehicles and then bear left to take the driveway of the rather nice Grange House. It is a delightful stretch of walking in summer. The driveway is lined with attractive wild flowers as you cross over a stream bridge and reach a lane. At the lane go left then, just past Woodford Cottage, go right through a hedge gap into a cultivated field. Cross the field towards the far left corner of the field aiming for the tower of All Saints Church in Trysull. At the field corner, go through a hand-gate and follow a hedged path to reach School Road – on the left is the **Plough Inn** if you are ready for refreshment.

Go right along School Road into **Trysull**. After passing by **All Saints Church**, go right into Bell Road then go left in front of the very attractive 'The Thatchers' cottage and walk along Trysull Holloway. Just after crossing a bridge over a stream, go right on a footpath which meanders below a flower-laden cottage to go over a stile into pastureland. At the field end, go over a further stile then bear left to ascend a cultivated field going beneath electric power lines to reach a lane corner. Proceed ahead and descend the lane passing Orchard Cottage on the left to reach **Awbridge Bridge** (bridge no 49).

Proceed over the old bridge and go right, descending to take the left bank of the **Staffordshire and Worcestershire Canal**. This is a pleasant canalside stretch of walking where ducks, moorhens and coots may keep you company. You pass a cricket pitch on the far bank just before reaching the moorings to the Bratch Locks – so many colourful narrowboats to admire.

Awbridge Bridge, on the Staffordshire and Worcestershire Canal

At the Bratch Locks you can enjoy one of the finest of the treasures along the Staffordshire and Worcestershire Canal. There can be no better summer pleasure in West Staffordshire than to see ornate narrowboats negotiate the amazing 30ft/9.2m locks – from the top there is a fine view down the valley with the spire of Wombourne Church set to the backdrop of the Orton Hills. Three locks set very close together by an attractive octagonal tollhouse combine to form a picture postcard sight – a much photographed scene and there are many visitors in summer.

WALK 16 – A Peatling Parva Meander

A gentle walk around attractive countryside in Leicestershire during which you will meander by a pleasing stream and pass the impressive building of Peatling Parva Hall.

Distance:	5 miles (8km)
Duration:	Allow 3 hours
Refreshments:	The Cock Inn, Peatling Magna, and the Joiners Arms, Bruntingthorpe
Walk Start:	Peatling Magna is 8½ miles (13.5km) south of Leicester. Leave Leicester on the A50 going right onto the A426 then left onto the B5366. In 2½ miles (4km) go left again onto local roads to reach Peatling Magna
Car Parking:	Park in the main street of Peatling Magna near the Cock Inn
Terrain:	Generally even walking in open countryside
OS Map:	Explorer 233 – Leicester and Hinckley

From the Cock Inn walk down Arnesby Lane opposite and in about 150m bear right to enter the churchyard of **All Saint's Church**. Walk to the left of the church building to go through a hand-gate at its rear. Now bear right across a field in a generally south direction via a sunken way and go over a field stile into a cultivated field. Maintain the same line over this field and you reach a stile onto the Peatling Parva road near to a road junction. At the junction bear left to go over a field corner stile to join the waymarked Leicestershire Round. Cross a cart-bridge over a series of stiles – there is a stream to your right which follows a similar line. As you enter the fourth field you see buildings at the field top left – one is an old telephone exchange.

Continue over a further stile in the bottom corner of the field near to the small stream. Walk close to the stream as you progress over the next three fields. Enter the third field via a bridle gate, but go right over a stile before you reach the field end (the Leicestershire Round continues ahead) and before a spinney on the right. Go past the spinney, now on your left, and at the stile ahead, go left and walk near to the fence on the left – the stream is still to your right and is now lined with attractive alder trees.

Peatling Hall

At the field end veer right to go over a further stile and a cart-bridge over the stream and near to an old brick **barn**. Now continue to the right of the stream and proceed over a couple of stiles and through a small plantation to arrive in the parkland to **Peatling Parva Hall**. Ensure that you keep to the footpath in the park. You pass to the front of the impressive hall near to a small and ornate lake area with attractive waterfalls – a pretty scene indeed. Llamas and sheep may well be seen in the park grounds.

After passing by the hall aim for the large conifer in the far right-hand field corner. You pass by two lovely white dwellings – one very finely thatched – and see St Andrew's Church, **Peatling Parva**, set back

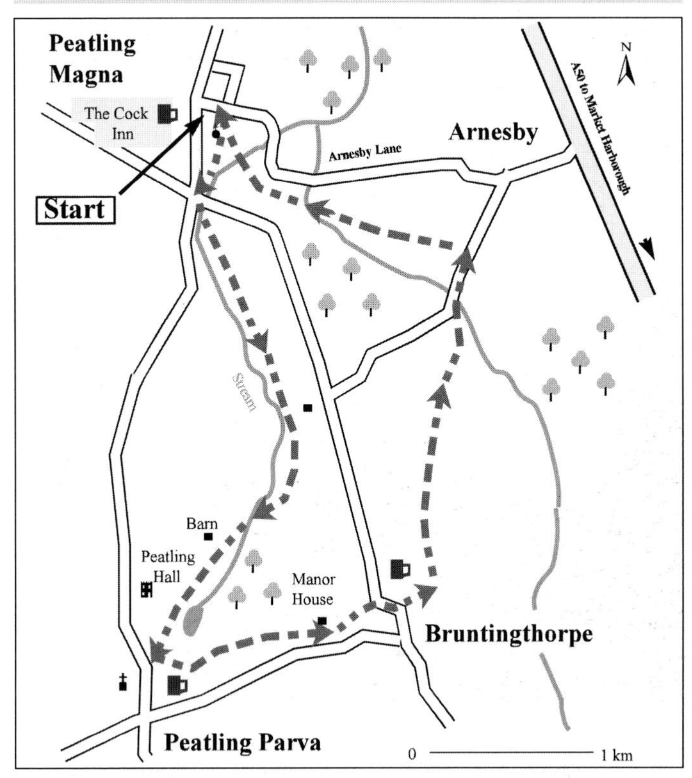

between the dwellings. Spare time to meander the small attractive village by walking an enclosed ditty path set to the left of the thatched white house. At the village road go left if you wish to visit the Shires pub. On the other side of the road a lane leads to the 14th-century **St Andrew's Church** which was restored in 1870. The perpendicular west tower has a frieze and battlements.

Return via the ditty path to the main walk and follow the sign to Bruntingthorpe by walking down the field to a field corner stile. Proceed over the stile and a footbridge maintaining the same walk line through plantations and cross a plank bridge over a stream. Ascend the next field, passing the end of the left hedge, to go generally east over a stile by a field gate. Maintain your walk line to a stile near the next field at the far right corner. Now go right and follow the field edge up to trees, a gate and a stile. Go over the stile and go left to proceed through a farm gate by a tall corrugated-iron shed (on the left) with farm sheds on the right. A stile by the next gate leads you to the driveway entrance to **Manor House** Farm in Bruntingthorpe.

Go right to reach a road where bear left over a stile to reach and pass to the left of the little church of **Bruntingthorpe**. Leave the churchyard via a kissing gate and follow a tarmac strip lane and along Church Walk to arrive in the middle of the village. You pass by the Joiners Arms and a superb thatched house on your left. Continue down the lane until you reach the main road and now go right past a corner garage. At the next road corner, go left and take Little End past some very attractive houses. At the end of the lane bend left to temporarily rejoin the Leicestershire Round passing a house called Staplecourt.

Bear left to go over a stile to the right of a farm gate but proceed ahead in a generally north direction to go over a stile. Now maintain this line over the next seven fields and waymarked stiles with the small stream on your left. Eventually the stream bends across the path and you bear right to go over a stile and aim for the far right corner of the second field and a big ash tree. Diagonally cross the next field and as you go over the hedge (parish boundary) you see a small brick building. Aim to the left of the building and cross a foot-plank to reach the Lutterworth road at a footpath sign.

Go right along the road towards Arnesby and at the pair of footpath signs go left over a stile to pass by a large barn on your way to the field end stile. Maintain your walk line over the next two fields and then aim for a midfield waymark sign. At the sign veer right to go over a further stile with the spire of Peatling Magna Church now clearly visible ahead. Aim for the spire as you diagonally cross the large field to yet another stile which leads to a final stile at the bottom of the field below the church. Ascend the field to go through the hand-gate into the churchyard and make your way up to the Cock Inn.

WALK 17 – A Long Mynd Walk

A superb hill walk over the Long Mynd ending with a stroll along gentle footpaths past some of the many attractive houses in Church Stretton.

Distance:	6 miles (9.6km)
Duration:	Allow 3½ to 4 hours
Refreshments:	A tea room near the National Trust car park and a number of refreshment houses in Church Stretton
Walk Start:	Church Stretton is 8 miles south of Shrewsbury. As you enter the main street in the town bear right and follow the signs to Carding Mill Valley
Car Parking:	National Trust pay and display car park in Carding Mill Valley (GR 441948)
Terrain:	Hilly with a couple of scrambles – generally good underfoot
OS Map:	Explorer 217 – The Long Mynd and Wenlock Edge

From the National Trust car park walk up **Carding Mill Valley**. You pass by the NT shop, some tea rooms and a final car park area before reaching the stone footpath that ascends between **Calf Ridge** and **Haddon Hill** (1533ft/467m). This is attractive walking in delightful scenery but do pause from time to time to enjoy a fine retrospective view down the valley.

When you reach a junction of paths, go right on a bridleway path (called Mott's Road) that ascends, arcing left between Calf Ridge and Haddon Hill. After about about 1 mile (1.6km) of ascent you reach the ridge of the Long Mynd at a junction of paths (at 1575ft/480m). Here, go right following the post way-sign to High Park and take a green hill-top track going east with heather all around you. After a short period the track arcs left and then straightens to a northeast direction. In about a further ½ mile/900m you reach a farm fence. Here, bear right to join

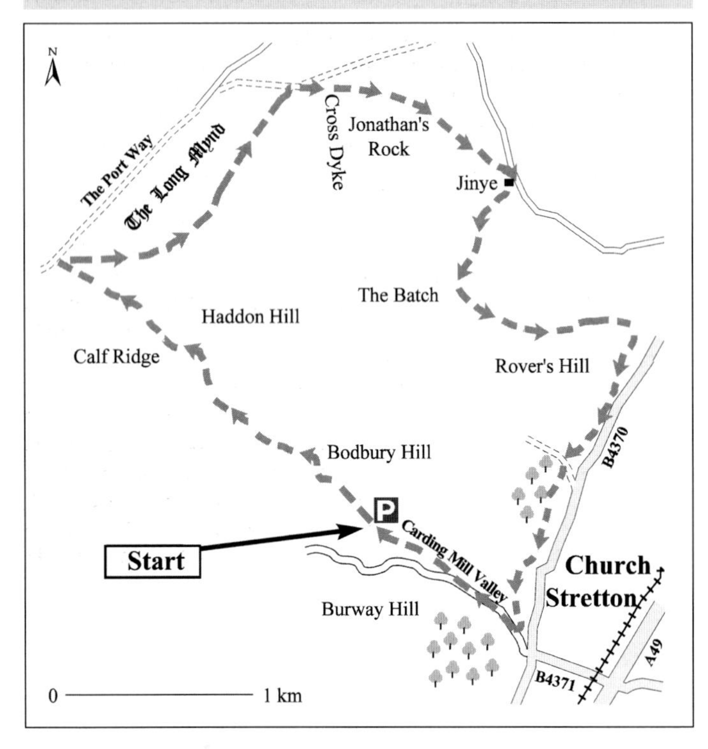

a path that soon arcs right again away from the fence path as you proceed generally east once again. This path is the start of your descent and after going over **Cross Dyke**, arcs right (southeast) to descend with Jonathan's Rock to your right. The clear footpath passes to the back of **Plush House**. Here, bear right onto a permissive footpath that continues to the left of a spring stream with an accommodation building, **Jinye**, to the left by the side of a lane.

Continue by following the waymark signs that lead left along the valley with Haddon Hill ahead. The path arcs left on a hill ledge which can involve a small scramble. It descends to go to the left of a wire fence with a valley cottage to the right below. Descend to the track/drive that leads to the cottage but go left to continue the descent. You pass by a small pool with a building in the small field to the right and then the track becomes a tarmac lane/drive. After going over a small bridge by a ford the lane arcs left, and ahead to the left you see some cottages. At the entrance to the cottages cross over the spring stream and ascend a clear path going right. This leads to a stile.

Go over the stile, bear right towards a half-timbered dwelling and go over a further stile onto a path at the rear of houses. Take this path, enjoying the occasional views over the houses towards Caradoc Hill (1625ft/459m), Helmett Hill and ahead Raglett Hill (1306ft/398m). You negotiate a couple of kissing gates after the second of which arc right to ascend away from the B4370 road. You pass a bench seat from which there is a fine view of Caradoc Hill and then descend to a kissing gate onto the lane to Cwmdale. Cross the lane and proceed through a gate opposite to continue along the pleasant path that now leads through trees and soon arrives on a residential road called Madeira Walk. Continue along the road of fine well-maintained houses (many with black and white half-timbered areas). You soon reach the road to **Carding Mill Valley**. Go right and stroll the quiet road to reach the NT car park.

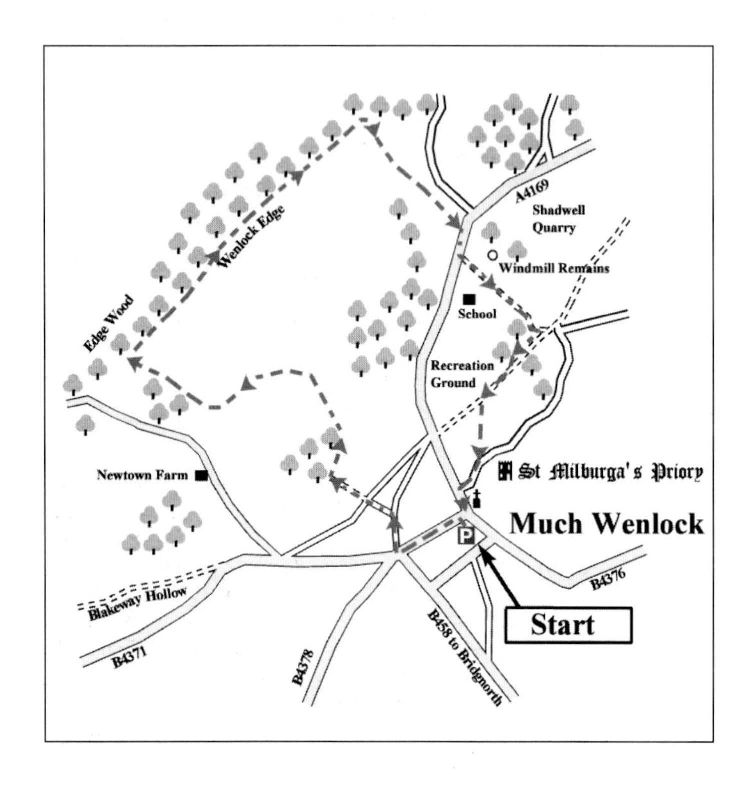

A4169
Shadwell
Quarry
Windmill Remains
Wenlock Edge
Edge Wood
School
Recreation
Ground
St Milburga's Priory
Much Wenlock
Newtown Farm
Blakeway Hollow
B4371
B4378
B458 to Bridgnorth
B4376
Start

WALK 18 – A Much Wenlock Experience

An easy walk in gentle Shropshire countryside. The walk embraces Wenlock Edge and offers an opportunity to visit the famous Wenlock Priory (English Heritage) and to meander through the attractive town of Much Wenlock.

Distance:	3 miles (4.8km)
Duration:	Allow 1½ to 2 hours
Refreshments:	Many establishments in Much Wenlock
Walk Start:	Much Wenlock is 8 miles northwest of Bridgnorth. The car park is on the left as you enter the town on the A458 road
Car Parking:	Pay and display car park (toilets) off Barrow Street in Much Wenlock
Terrain:	Easy walking
OS Map:	Explorer 217 – The Long Mynd and Wenlock Edge

From the car park walk the covered footpath into the High Street which is almost opposite the Corn Exchange building. Go left and down the attractive High Street (formerly known as Spittle Street on Hospital Street – named after the Hospital of St John that stood on the site of the present Corn Exchange) of **Much Wenlock**. To the right you pass by the 17th-century Raynald's Mansion, and on the left is the 14th-century Talbot Inn. After progressing past Back Lane you pass Ashfield Hall. Just past King Street is the Squatters Cottage – a 17th-century dwelling with a wonderful outside chimney stack.

Raynald's Mansion *is a magnificent half-timbered hall, the ground floor occupied as an antique shop.*

Ashfield Hall *is a fine large 16th-century town house formerly known as The Ash. In 1642 it was the 'Blew Bridge' inn and Charles I stayed there en route to the Battle of Edgehill.*

At the road junction with the B4378 Ludlow road and opposite the Gaskell Arms, go right and along the pavement of Smithfield Road. In about 150m go left and walk up Bridge Road, proceeding along a footpath to the left of the old bridge. Cross over Southfield Road and continue up a clear track and in 200m you reach woodland. Bear slightly right, enter the woodland and go right to take a clear footpath along the edge of the trees.

Exit the woodland following the waymarker of Jack Myton's Way to cross a cultivated field with a hedge on your right. At the field end proceed through a hedge gap (once a hand-gate) and then go left to take a wide path with the hedge now on your left. Continue along the path over two cultivated fields – to your left you see some shiny grain silos on Newtown Farm. Shortly after the path arcs right, you cross over a farm track and continue on the path to the left of a field hedge until you reach **Edge Wood**.

Go right and take the clear footpath to the right of the wood – this is **Wenlock Edge** and you will enjoy a pleasant valley view to the right. Take this footpath for about the next ¾ mile (1.2km), when the path arcs right and you enter the trees briefly – ahead is a nice view and

The Guildhall at Much Wenlock

you see the cooling towers of the power station by the River Severn at Ironbridge Gorge. Exit the wood via a stile and proceed right now walking to the left of the field hedge. After going over a couple of fields and stiles you reach the A4169 road via a hand-gate.

Go right along the pavement of the A4169 for about 100m, then cross over with care. Proceed through a hand-gate opposite and ascend a path to reach a ruined **windmill** – you will enjoy the pleasing view over the valley to Ash Coppice set on the hill. Descend on the other side of the windmill and proceed through a farm gate. The path arcs left and descends via steps to a dismantled railway line. Cross the former line and ascend the steps opposite to arrive in a quiet narrow lane. Go right and along this lane. To your left is that pleasing view and soon there will be parkland to your right. The lane passes by St Milburga's Priory and you have the opportunity to visit this fine English Heritage property – founded in the 17th century, the monastery is worth a visit.

Continue up the lane past Priory Hall (built by public subscription as a National School in 1848) to reach Bull Ring (bull-baiting took place here for hundreds of years). Note the savings bank door and the old police station. Go left into Wilmore Street and on your left you pass Holy Trinity Church and then the superb half-timbered 16th-century **Guildhall**. The Guildhall was built in 1878 as a market hall but today contains the Much Wenlock Museum and the tourist information centre (in the museum building opposite).

Go right into the High Street and then left through the archway to return to the car park.

WALK 19 – Historic Birmingham and the Canals

An easy walk along stretches of the towpaths of the canals in the centre of Birmingham together with a visit to the jewellery quarter of this great city. The return route takes you through the old centre of the city where you pass by the superb civic and municipal buildings. An opportunity for a pleasant day in England's second city.

Distance:	3½ miles (5.6km)
Duration:	Allow a full day to explore Birmingham
Refreshments:	Many pubs and tea rooms by the canalside and along the route
Walk Start:	When approaching the city from the A38, Bristol Street, proceed over Holloway Circus into Suffolk Queensway. Holiday Street car park is on the left
Car Parking:	Pay and display car park off Holiday Street
Terrain:	Easy walking mainly on canal towpaths
OS Map:	A city street map and information can be obtained from: Visitor information centre, 130 Colmore Row, Birmingham, West Midlands B3 3AP (Tel. 0121 693 6300)

From the car park, proceed down Holiday Street and go right into Bridge Street. Cross over the left side of the street and you pass the Warf (Beefeater) pub to reach the entrance to Gas Street Basin. Descend the steps to the left of the Basin and cross over the Worcestershire and Birmingham Canal. Now go right along the path which leads beneath the Bristol Street Tunnel to arrive in Water's Edge. To the left is Brindley Place where there is a good selection of eating houses and then the fantastic National Sea Life Centre.

Continue along the left bank passing beneath Sheepcote Street bridge to reach the St Vincent Bridge. Pass beneath this bridge and ascend the other side to cross over the bridge. Now descend to take the path on the other side of the Birmingham Main Line Canal. Initially you walk past narrowboats moored by the canal edge until you arrive at Old

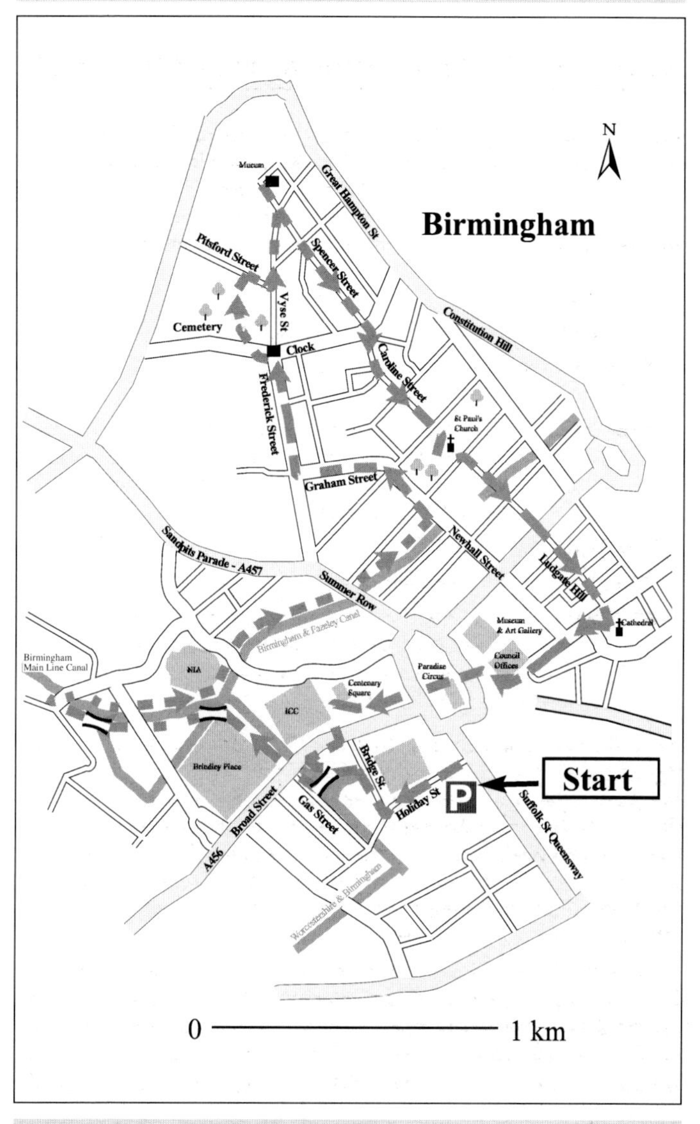
Birmingham
N
Museum
Great Hampton St
Pitsford Street
Spencer Street
Vyse St
Cemetery
Clock
Constitution Hill
Caroline Street
Frederick Street
St Paul's Church
Graham Street
Sandpits Parade - A457
Summer Row
Newhall Street
Ludgate Hill
Cathedral
Museum & Art Gallery
Birmingham & Fazeley Canal
Birmingham Main Line Canal
NIA
Paradise Circus
Council Offices
Centenary Square
ICC
Brindley Place
Bridge St
Holiday St
Start
Broad Street
A456
Gas Street
Suffolk St Queensway
Worcestershire & Birmingham
0
1 km

Turn Junction, where the Worcestershire and Birmingham, the Birmingham Main Line and the Birmingham and Frazeley canals all meet.

Bear left at the junction to continue on the left bank of the Birmingham and Frazeley Canal passing the National Indoor Arena building and with a fine view ahead of the very tall British Telecom Tower. You pass by a series of lock gates to reach the Canning Walk and a number of arches. Ascend steps under the road bridge signed 'Jewellery Quarter' to arrive in **Newhall Street**.

Go left and take the pavement along Newhall Street and into **Graham Street**. Continue to the main road and go right along **Frederick Street** passing the Argent Centre and with the Jewellery Quarter Clock Tower ahead. At the clock, go left into Warstone Lane then just after passing the gateway to the Warstone Lane Cemetery, go right up a pathway into the cemetery. As you proceed through the cemetery you pass by the Catacombs to arrive in Pitsford Street. Now go right and walk up to **Vyse Street** and you are in the Jewellery Quarter. Go left along Vyse Street, pausing to see the multitude of jewellery premises. At the end of Vyse Street is the Jewellery Discovery Centre but you go right along Spencer Street passing by the Jeweller's Arms and proceeding towards the City Centre.

Canal signs

At the end of Spencer Street bear right into Caroline Street crossing over the road to enter the churchyard of the superb **St Paul's Church**. Leave the churchyard of St Paul's and walk along Ludgate Hill. Proceed over the Birmingham and Frazeley Canal with the BT Tower to the right and cross the footbridge over Great Charles Street Queensway. There are a number of fine old buildings (including the

The museum and town hall

former Birmingham and Midland Eye Hospital – 1833) to admire as you continue up Church Street to arrive in Colmore Row opposite the massive Birmingham **Cathedral**.

Continue by walking along Colmore Row and you soon reach Victoria Square – what a magnificent sight – with the amazing building of the Museum and Art Gallery/Town Hall and Council House with children playing in summer in the water fountains. Bear right and continue into Paradise Forum with the Central Library to the right. Cross over the walkway into Centenary Square where you pass by the Repertory Theatre, the Hull of Memory and the ICC buildings. On arrival in Broad Street, go right and in about 100m go right to descend to the Worcestershire and Birmingham Canal and the Gas Street Basin. Now retrace your steps to the Holiday Street car park.

WALK 20 – A Meriden Woodland Walk

A pleasant woodland walk around the very centre of England. In spring the woods are filled with lovely bluebells.

Distance:	6 miles (9.6km)
Duration:	Allow 3 to 3½ hours
Refreshments:	The Queen's Head pub, in a convenient position on the Heart of England Way, is a regular eating place for walkers
Walk Start:	Meriden is 5½ miles (9km) west of Coventry. From the A45 go left onto the B4104 into Meriden. The Queen's Head is set to the right and is reached via an access road
Car Parking:	Park by the roadside opposite the Queen's Head (GR 252821)
Terrain:	Easy walking on good paths and on fairly level ground
OS Map:	Explorer 221 – Coventry and Warwick

From the Queen's Head pub in Meriden, proceed up Walsh Lane and in about 300m go right (with **Village Farm** on your right) to take a narrow lane which in a further 400m dips beneath the main A45 Birmingham–Coventry road. Continue along the lane into **Eaves Green**.

In the village you pass by a **caravan park** and then go left over a stile onto a track which leads through the fine woodland of **Meriden Shafts**. The woods contain a wide variety of wild flowers and, in spring, are well known in the area for bluebells. Proceed over a second stile then walk over two more fields and enter trees over a further stile. Take the lovely path through the woods and go over a stile at its end. Now go left then right onto a clear track to walk by the hedge of three fields and to go over a stile onto Harvest Hill Lane in **Hollyberry End**.

Go left past **Ivy House Farm** and take the lane for about 300m, then where the lane bends left go right over a stile to diagonally cross a field to a stile/footbridge in its far left corner. Continue by taking the track on

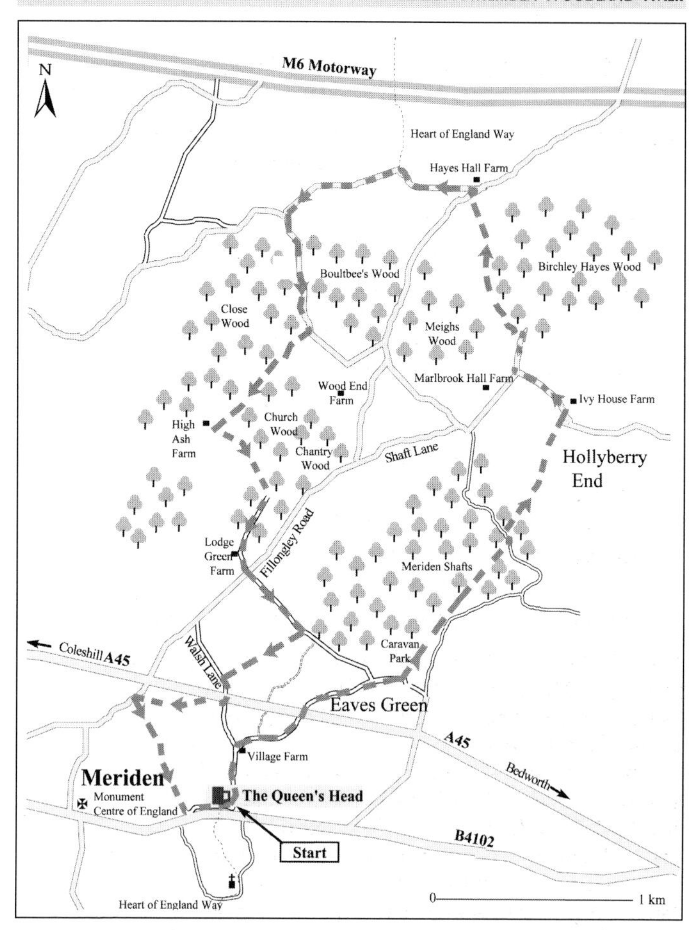

the edge of **Birchley Hayes Wood** then aim to go over a stile set to the left of **Hayes Hall Farm** ahead.

Go left along the Fillongley Road and leave the Heart of England Way which goes right into pastureland. Walk along the quiet lane for about ¾ mile (1.2km) and ahead to your left you see a communication mast. Fifty yards/metres after passing the mast, go right through a hedge gap to take a clear path set to the left of **Close Wood**. You enter the wood via a further stile and can then enjoy a delightful stretch of woodland walking. In spring the bluebells form a delightful blue carpet as you exit the woods.

Exit Close Wood and take the clear path over cultivated land to reach **High Ash Farm** and a farm track/lane. Go left and descend the track/lane in a southeast direction. Go over the stile by the locked gate and bear right to descend a lane going past **Lodge Green Farm** to reach the Fillongley road. Cross over the main road and continue down Lodge Green Lane opposite for about 350m. Now go right over a stile to walk in open land on a clear path which follows a line of oak trees – a pleasant stretch of walking which soon ends as you near the noisy A45 road. At the end of the large field go left along the lane to cross over the **A45**. At the end of the bridge, go right over a stile to walk a diversion path high above the A45.

Walking through the Close Wood

In 100m go left over a stile into pastureland and aim for a footbridge set to the right of a pond surrounded by trees. From the footbridge ascend the next field going east to a pair of corner field stiles. Now bear sharp left over the second stile to descend over several fields in a southeast direction. As you descend into the town of **Meriden** the view of the hill-top church impresses. Aim to the left of a row of newish bungalows and go over a stile onto the access road to the Queen's Head. Go left to return to your car.

WALK 21 – Kinver Canal Walk

After an initial short steep ascent up to the landmark of St Peter's Church, this easy scenic walk follows the towpath of the delightful Staffordshire and Worcester-shire Canal between Kinver and Stewponey Locks – the River Stour runs next to the canal. A short stretch of field-walking then leads into a pretty bluebell wood by the side of the meandering River Stour and there are pleasant views as you return along the fascinating High Street of the village of Kinver.

Distance:	5 miles (8km)
Duration:	Allow 2½ hours
Refreshments:	Several attractive pubs in the village of Kinver. The walk passes the Vine Inn which is by Kinver Lock on the banks of the Staffordshire and Worcestershire Canal
Walk Start:	Kinver is about 5 miles west of Stourbridge. From Stourbridge take the A458 road towards Bridgnorth. Go left at Stourton onto the A449 and take the next right into Kinver
Car Parking:	Public car park at the rear of the post office in High Street, Kinver (GR 846833)
Terrain:	Easy walking along the canal towpath and on good footpaths
OS Map:	Explorer 219 – Wolverhampton and Dudley

The historic village of Kinver is renowned as a centre for leisure walking and riding with Kinver Edge, to the south, being a well-known walking area in the Midlands. It comprises some 200 acres of superb scenery and views and is a favourite beauty spot in the southwest corner of Staffordshire. Prior to 1066, Kinver and neighbouring Stourton belonged to Algar, Alderman of Mercia, but was forfeited to the crown in 1070. The village appears in Domesday Book under the name of Chenevare and there are a number of buildings of interest to enjoy. St Peter's Church on the hill above Kinver has a unique 'stained-glass window' lampshade

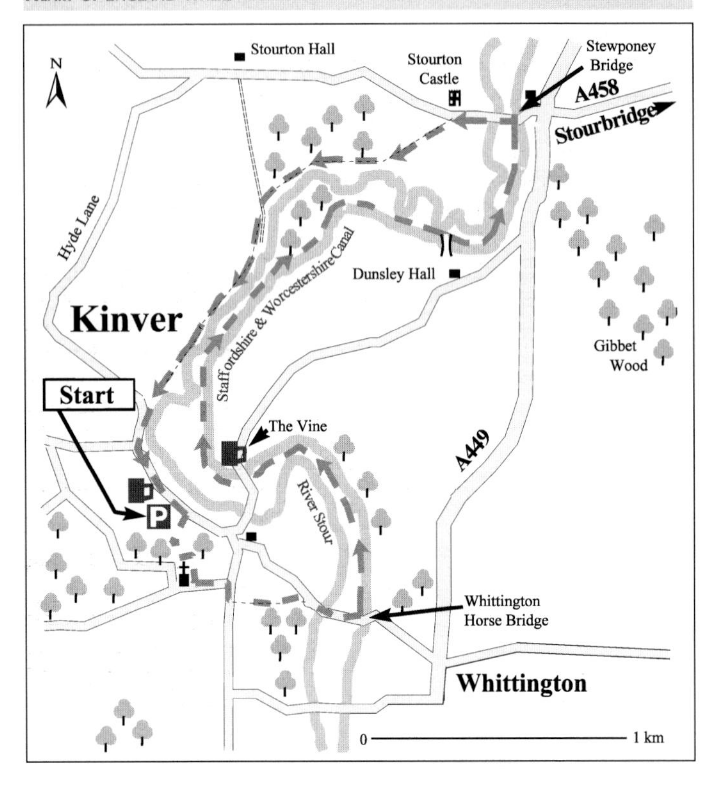

and contains a fascinating display history of Kinver. The medieval High Street contains many interesting buildings – the White Hart Hotel and the Pharmacy are two of the buildings which helped the village win an Architectural Heritage Award in 1975. Kinver Grammar School in Dark Lane, near St Peter's Church, is a superb 16th-century half-timbered building now occupied as a private house. At the beginning of the 20th century, the promotional literature for the tramway christened Kinver area 'The Switzerland of the Midlands'. It is a pretty village.

From the car park at the rear of the High Street, ascend the steep zigzag path at the back of the car park to visit **St Peter's Church** on the hill –

there is a fine view from the churchyard wall to enjoy and the church is worth a visit if only to see its unique 'stained-glass window'.

Exit the churchyard via the attractive lychgate and bear left to reach a lane. Go left again and descend the hill to Kinver Hill road. Now go right along the edge of the quiet road for some 70m, then cross over and proceed through a kissing gate onto a fenced path that soon leads to a second kissing gate and open fields. Take the footpath to the right of the field hedge and at the field corner bear slightly left to descend the cultivated field to a kissing gate onto Dark Lane. Now go right and stroll the lane past some attractive houses. You soon pass the Anchor Hotel and Restaurant where bear right to take a fenced lane until you reach the banks of James Brindley's **Staffordshire and Worcestershire Canal**. Go left under a canal bridge and follow the towpath of the contour canal going initially north. In the days of the Industrial Revolution you would have passed several forges and steel mills hammering and blazing away their products, but today the scene is of peace and serenity with colourful canal barges either moored or meandering the attractive canal.

Continue along the towpath to Kinver Lock Bridge – the **Vine Inn** by the bridge is a very popular local pub. After passing the busy Kinver Lock (no 29) you reach a mooring area where many brightly painted barges puff out smoke from their chimneys during the spring and autumn months. The River Stour is close on your left, weaving in and out, appearing to want to collide with the canal but then veering away into the countryside below Kinver.

In about ½ mile/1km you arrive at Hyde Lock (no 30).

It was above this lock that the first commercially successful iron slitting mill in England was built in 1629 by Richard Foley. It was powered by the River Stour during the Industrial Revolution and in 1860 peaked its production at a time when the population of the village had reached 3551. Production ceased in the 1880s and, sadly, Hyde Mill became derelict in 1912. The building has long disappeared although the footings of the mill structures and the boundary walls are still visible today. Just past Hyde Lock, molehills on the hill bank opposite form a pleasing picture to a backdrop of conifer trees.

Continue along the towpath passing through the 25m Dunsley Tunnel.

Near here in 1805 the Squire of Dunsley Hall was waylaid by a highwayman as he returned from selling cattle at Kidderminster market. He was left for dead but managed to crawl back to Dunsley Hall where he died. The highwayman was caught in nearby Whittington Inn and was the last man to be publicly hanged and gibbeted at Gibbet Wood, situated about ½ mile/1km to the east.

Stewponey Bridge

Just before you walk beneath **Stewponey Bridge** the towpath again draws very close to the River Stour and soon you arrive at Stewponey Lock (no 31).

Note the tollhouse to the right. It is now little more than a souvenir shop but was a very busy tollhouse in the 1930s when as many as 800 vessels registered each half year. The Stewponey Inn is reputed to have derived its name from Estepona – birthplace of a Spanish bride who was brought to England by one of Wellington's soldiers after the Peninsular War.

You can cross over the canal lock gate if you wish to visit the former tollhouse or merely pause to admire and photograph the fine old lock buildings – it makes a most attractive picture. Leave the lock area going right to take the pavement over the River Stour bridge.

In about 200m you reach the castellated gate entrance to **Stourton Castle**.

The castle, which was held for the roundheads in 1644 (there remains a hole in a wooden door made by a cannon ball of this period), has a Gothic lodge, a symmetrical façade and a castellated tower (Pevsner 1974). Its chequered past reveals a fascinating history and was once the home of the Foley family but is now in private ownership.

Here, go left through a kissing gate onto a clear path over a cultivated field and enjoy a fine countryside view before going over a field stile into woodland. The path follows a wire fence and in the spring you walk between carpets of beautiful bluebells to emerge eventually by Hyde Farm cottages. Proceed along the clear path over pastureland passing through a series of kissing gates with the River Stour close on your left. This delightful stretch of walking provides a fine view of St Peter's Church which overlooks Kinver from the hill ahead.

Continue by walking between some leisure buildings and the bowling green/miniature railway and then ascend a tarmac lane to turn left along the High Street of this attractive village of period buildings.

WALK 22 – Stokesay Castle Visit

A pleasant stroll through typical Shropshire countryside with lovely views and the opportunity to visit the most magnificent Stokesay Castle.

Distance:	3½ miles (5.6km)
Duration:	Allow 2 hours
Refreshments:	The Craven Arms Hotel
Walk Start:	The Craven Arms Hotel is about 6 miles (9.5km) north of Ludlow on the A49 road
Car Parking:	Park by the roadside in Craven Arms near the Craven Arms Hotel or in its car park by arrangement with the proprietor (GR 435825)
Terrain:	Generally easy walking on good footpaths
OS Map:	Explorer 217 – The Long Mynd and Wenlock Edge

From the Craven Arms Hotel follow the pavement of the Ludlow road (A49) for 200m. After passing the fire station and an antiques showroom, go right into Dodd's Lane. The lane leads beneath a railway bridge where it becomes a track. After going over a stile bear left and take a footpath which hugs the left field hedge as you proceed over four fields, going over three stiles and a gate. There are hazelnut bushes in the hedge and a pleasant view to the right embraces Sallow Coppice. The path arcs generally left and in the middle of the next field you meet a clear path coming from the right.

Go left along this path aiming south for a corner field stile near to a white **cottage** at **Clapping Wicket**. Now bear left to join a forest type track which leads into **Stoke Wood**. This delightful green track is a blaze of wildflower colour in summer. After walking the track for some 600m go left to leave the track and the woods over a stile into pastureland. A beautiful scene greets you with the superb Stokesay Castle set to the backdrop of the Shropshire hills. Descend the clear path over four fields with the castle getting ever large as you approach the main railway line

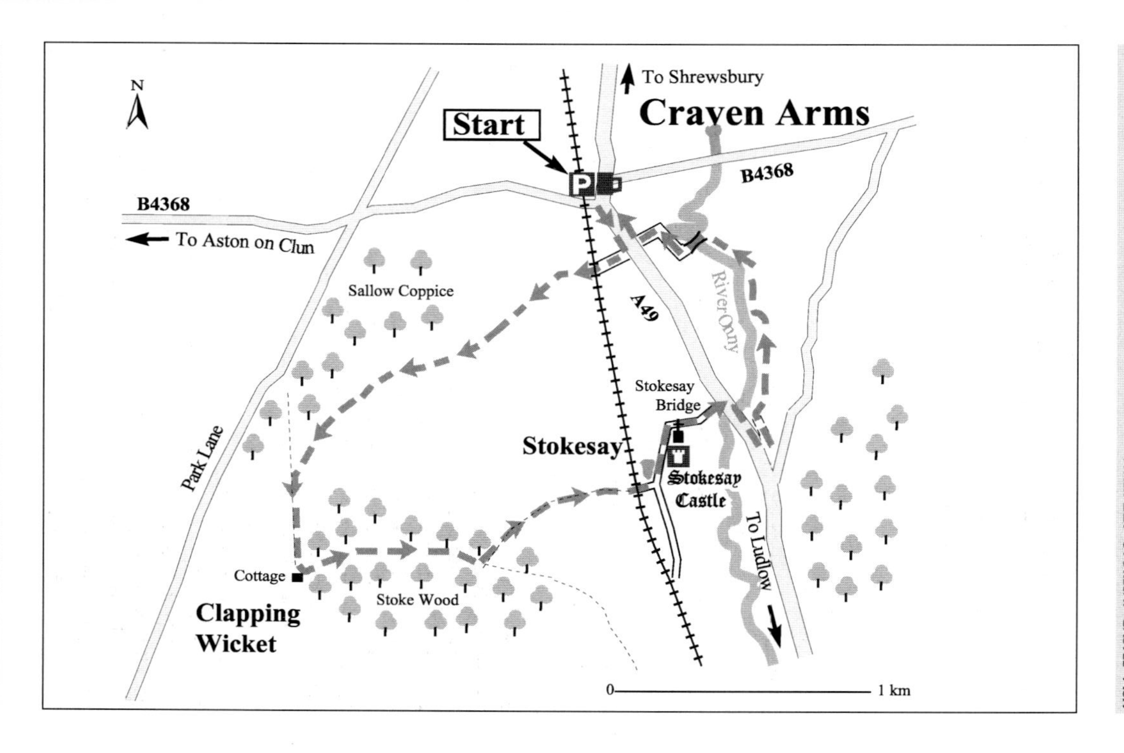
N
Start
To Shrewsbury
Craven Arms
B4368
B4368
To Aston on Clun
Sallow Coppice
A49
River Onny
Stokesay Bridge
Stokesay
Stokesay Castle
To Ludlow
Park Lane
Cottage
Stoke Wood
Clapping Wicket
0
1 km

over stiles. Take care crossing the line for they really are express trains. Take a farm lane to the left before going through a final gate onto Castle Lane.

Go left and walk past **Stokesay Castle** building. Entrance to this English Heritage castle can be made through the churchyard of the church of St John the Baptist. Spare time to visit:

Right Tower, Stokesay Castle

***St John the Baptist Church** was built as a chapel to the castle, in about 1150. This interesting building, which served the community Craven Arms until the 21st century, is a rare example of church activity in Puritan times. It has a lovely 17th-century gallery which was used by musicians and songsters until about 1855 and under this there are five primitive pews which escaped the Civil War.*

*The 13th-century **Stokesay Castle** is one of the finest fortified manor houses in England. Its earliest occupants were the de Sayes who fortified the building from Welsh marauders. The attractive right tower has been surmounted by a 16th-century half-timbered storey and there is a great gabled banqueting hall with tall gothic* *windows. The black and white Elizabethan gatehouse catches the eye and offers a fine photo opportunity.*

Continue along the lane past the car park and walk to the A49 road. Go right across **Stokesay Bridge** over the River Onny and cross over to the other side of the road. In 100m go left down a disused length of road. At its end, go right to descend steps and to take the riverside path back to Craven Arms town. This is a pretty stretch of walking above the small attractive river. After going over a couple of stiles the path arcs left over a stream footbridge and then a white metal footbridge over the Onny. You enter the town in a road called Newton. Go right and along the pavement past some attractive old half-timbered buildings. The Old Rectory is particularly nice. At the road end, go left and take School Road and you soon reach the A49 Ludlow road where go right and along the pavement back towards the Craven Arms Hotel.

Craven Arms is a small quiet market town apparently named after its large modernised Georgian inn. Sheep auctions take place between August and late October and it is then that the town comes to life.

WALK 23 – The Clent Hills Clamber

A fine hill walk with attractive views in all directions. There is the opportunity to visit a picturesque Norman church where a historic silence pervades.

Distance:	4¾ miles (7.6km)
Duration:	Allow 2¾ hours
Refreshments:	The Hill Tavern, Clent
Walk Start:	Clent is about 8 miles (13km) northwest of Bromsgrove. From junction 4A of the M5 proceed northwest up the A491 road towards Stourbridge. In just under 4 miles (6.5km) go left and follow the signs towards Clent. Go ahead at the crossroads in Clent, up St Kenelm's Pass and then left up Adams Hill
Car Parking:	Free parking in the lane called Adams Hill near the Hill Tavern (GR 931796)
Terrain:	Hilly walking on mainly good footpaths. In wet weather some parts in the south may be muddy
OS Map:	Explorer 219 – Wolverhampton and Dudley

From the parking area walk up **Adams Hill** passing by Four Stones Restaurant. Go right at Hill Tavern and take the clear wide stone track past a house for a fine valley view, then arc left and descend steeply. Just before a path junction go right down a footpath which descends a stepped path into woodland. Keep to the right edge of the woodland. The track reduces to a footpath and then at a junction of tracks/paths, go right and descend a path. The path leads behind houses to arrive at the road in **Clent** opposite St Leonard's Church. Cross over the road and enter the churchyard. After visiting the church exit via the front lychgate onto a lane (signed to Walton Pool).

Go left and take the lane going southeast – you pass the Old School (on the right) and then the entrance to Clent Hall on the left. The gardens of Clent Hall are ablaze with beautiful rhododendrons in

The final approach to Stokesay Castle (Walk 22)

The impressive Ludlow Castle (Walk 25)

Fishermen on the River Severn near Bewdley Bridge (Walk 27)

The Stratford Canal at Bridge 48, Preston Bagot (Walk 31)

spring. Just past the hall gardens go left through a pair of kissing gates to reach a narrow lane. Proceed along the lane which becomes a residential drive – there are some very attractive large houses up to the left. Where the drive veers left to the house at **Walton Pool** go right over a stile and walk through a horse paddock to a second stile onto a lane. Cross over the lane and proceed over a further stile and walk across pastureland. There are fine views to the right that include the Malvern Hills.

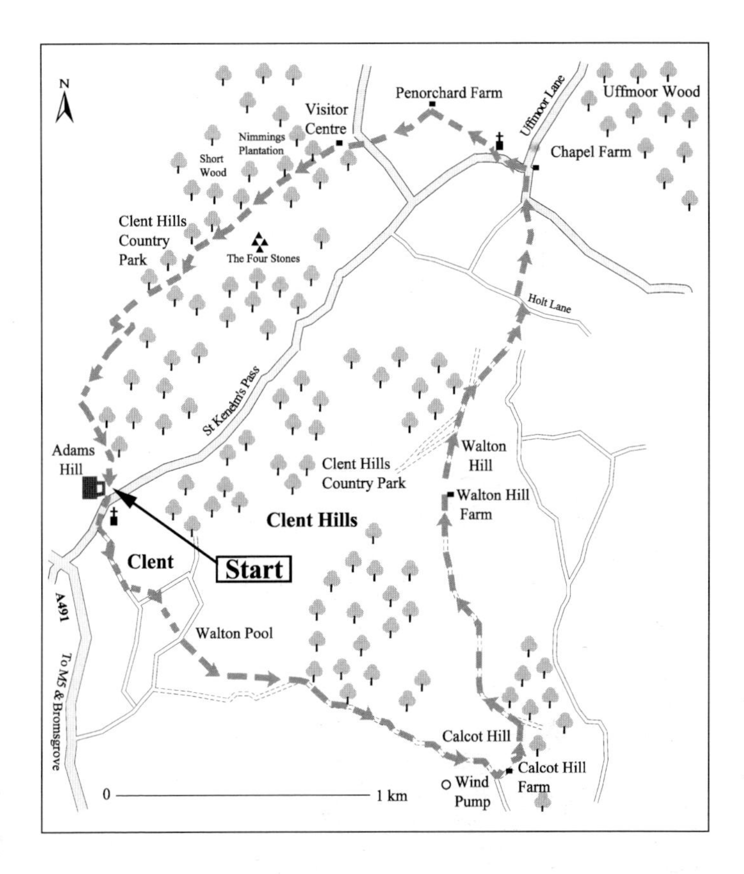

Continue over three fields and stiles passing by Walton Farm (to the right) and aiming for the bottom corner of woodland ahead. Go over the corner stile and bear left to continue along a good hedged farm track along the bottom of the woodland. Take this track for some 900m. You pass a wind pump and enjoy the regular fine views to the right. As you approach the farm lane by **Colcott Hill Farm**, go left over a stile by a large boulder.

Boulder from Arenig Mountain in North Wales brought here by the Welsh Ice Sheet in the Glacial Period.

Proceed on the path around the farm buildings. Go over a further stile and go left to join the North Worcestershire Path. This fine path hugs the hill top as it meanders northwards initially through an oak tree plantation and with a delightful valley view towards Romsley. After passing to the right of **Walton Hill Farm** via a stile bear left to ascend into the **Clent Hills Country Park** on a wide path/track. You will be welcomed by a fine panoramic view to the south and then as you reach the AA topograph (1034ft/315m) the view to the north embracing Dudley and Birmingham reveals itself.

Just before the topograph, bear right onto a footpath that descends northeast through an avenue of wild flowers. At **Holt Lane**, go left past the road junction, then go right over a stile to descend a large field aiming for a further stile in the bottom left corner. Enjoy the view ahead as you descend and then reach a road corner by the entrance to the Wesleys. Continue ahead for 110m then go left into Chapel Lane by **Chapel Farm**. In 100m enter the churchyard of St Kenelm's Church and visit this historic building.

St Kenelm's Norman Church was once the heart of the medieval village of Kenelmstone at a time when there was an inn (the Red Crow) plus some 30 wattle and daub houses. The church was a major centre for pilgrimages but sadly the village declined with the reformation and cessation of pilgrimages to St Kenelm's Well (still to be seen to the east of the church). The place where the spring rises is said to mark the spot where Kenelm, Prince of Mercia, was murdered and buried in about AD 820. St. Kenelm's Church is only open on Saturdays (2–5pm) between Easter and Harvest Festival and on Sundays in July.

Walk around the back of the church and exit the churchyard via a stile to take a footpath over fields going generally northwest. At the next stile go left and then bear right of **Penorchard Farm** ascending to a stile onto Hagley Wood Lane.

The four stones, on top of the Clent Hills

Cross over the lane and take the entrance drive to the **Nimmings Visitor Centre** (toilets). Proceed southwest on a bridle-way along the top of **Nimmings Plantation**. After about 300m of attractive woodland walking (the view to the right embraces the obelisk on Wychbury Hill) you re-enter the **Clent Hills Country Park**. To the left is a topographical viewing place. Pause here to enjoy a most superb view.

On a clear day the view embraces the Malverns (26 miles/42km) with the Herefordshire and Worcestershire Beacons clearly visible; the Black Mountains (52 miles/84km); Radnor Forest (47 miles/76km); Kinver Edge (7 miles/11km); Wenlock Edge (27 miles/43km); the Wrekin (26 miles/42km) and Cannock Chase (22 miles/35km). A little further to the left visit the Four Stones and topograph (998ft/304m) – and enjoy the view to the north.

From the topograph descend the main track going southwest. After about 600m of fine hill descent – the wonderful view will mesmerise – you see the Hill Tavern through the trees to the right below and can descend for refreshments near to where your car is parked.

WALK 24 – Baddesley Clinton Classic Walk

A delightful stroll along the side of the Grand Union Canal passing through attractive Warwickshire countryside along the Heart of England Way. There is the opportunity to visit the most beautiful Baddesley Clinton Manor (National Trust) and the amazing series of nine lock gates at Kingswood.

Distance:	4½ miles (7.2km) or 7¼ miles (11.6km) plus a further 2 miles (3km) to see the Kingswood Lock Gates
Duration:	Allow 2½ hours or 3¾ hours plus a further hour for the Kingswood Lock Gates
Refreshments:	The Navigation Inn is a pleasant canalside pub which welcomes walkers
Walk Start:	Baddesley Clinton is southeast of Solihull near the B4439 Hockley Heath–Rowington road. The Navigation Inn is set on the roadside near Kingswood Brook (GR 191279)
Car Parking:	The Navigation Inn has a large car park and customers are welcome to park their cars here while walking
Terrain:	Easy walking on the canal towpath and good footpaths
OS Map:	Explorer 220 – Birmingham; Explorer 221 – Coventry–Warwick

From the Navigation Inn car park go right to cross the Kingswood Bridge (bridge no 65) over the Grand Union Canal. Cross over the road and descend to the towpath of the canal. Go left under the bridge and take the canalside footpath going north for the next 1½ miles (2.5km). If you start the walk in the morning you will enjoy superb canal reflections. You pass beneath **Rising Bridge** (bridge no 66) and a fine pipe bridge before passing a well-maintained farm complex as you leave the canal at Turnover Bridge (bridge no 67).

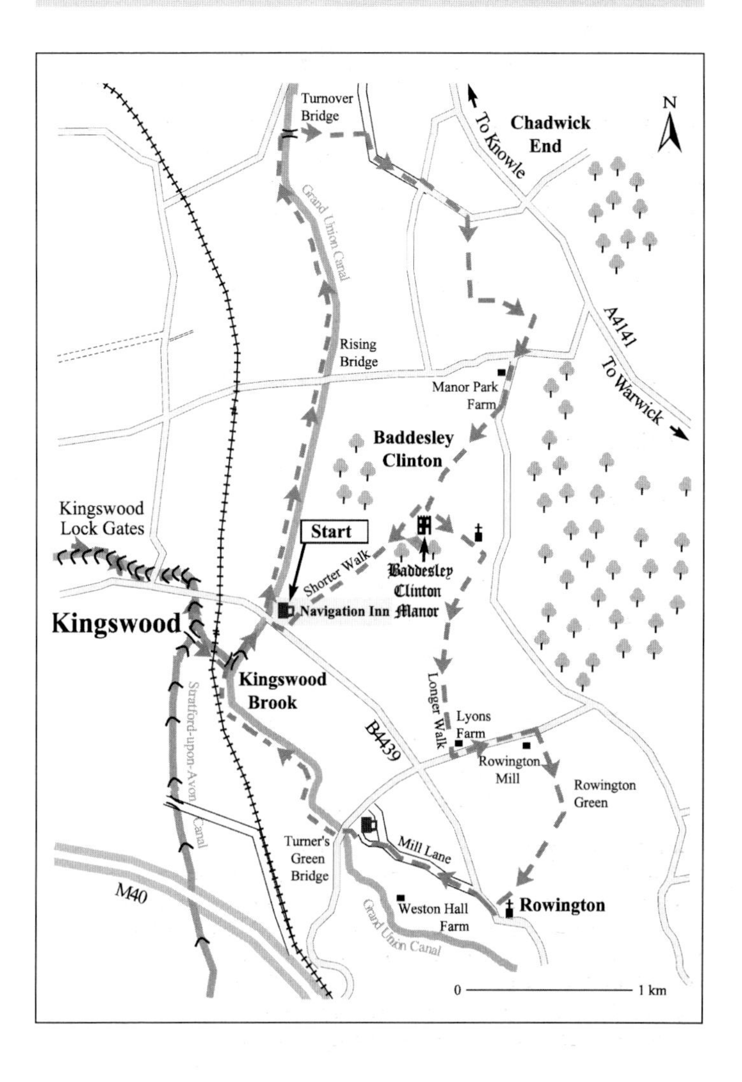

Turnover Bridge
Chadwick End
To Knowle
N
Grand Union Canal
A4141
To Warwick
Rising Bridge
Manor Park Farm
Baddesley Clinton
Kingswood Lock Gates
Start
Shorter Walk
Baddesley Clinton Manor
Navigation Inn
Kingswood
Kingswood Brook
Stratford-upon-Avon Canal
B4439
Longer Walk
Lyons Farm
Rowington Mill
Rowington Green
Turner's Green Bridge
Mill Lane
M40
Weston Hall Farm
Grand Union Canal
Rowington
0
1 km

Cross over **Turnover Bridge** and proceed east over a stile into pastureland. Then go over a smart gated footbridge and walk to the right of a field hedge until you veer right onto a hedged farm track. You leave the track via a stile at a junction of lanes which you cross and continue southeast along Netherwood Lane opposite. In about 200m, just before the first (large) house on the right, go right over a stile and follow a hedged/fenced path going generally south. You go over two more stiles then go left to walk by the field hedge until you reach a wide green bridlepath.

Go left (southeast) along this track for some 350m negotiating a couple of stiles then bearing right to join the Heart of England Way by the gates to Convent Farm. Take the drive of the converted convent to reach Rising Lane on the edge of the village of Baddesley Clinton**.** Go right at the lane and then at the next lane corner bear left at a road sign 'Mousley End 2, Hay Wood 1' and walk past the very modern **Manor Park Farm**. In 300m, just before the main entrance to Bromes Park, go right over stiles and continue on the Heart of England Way on a hedged path which circles the park perimeter, passing in and out of attractive woodland before reaching the entrance drive (NT) to **Baddesley Clinton Manor** via a small kissing gate. Do spare time to visit the beautiful manor, its fine gardens and the attractive village church.

Shorter Walk

Continue by crossing over the entrance drive and leave the Heart of England Way over the stile opposite to enter the parkland of the manor. The impressive moated building offers an intriguing vista to your left as you continue to the right of trees and you get glimpses of the gardens and maybe the superb small lake through the trees. After going over a stile at the bottom of the trees, the path proceeds southeast by a field hedge with pleasant views over Kingswood to the right. At the field stile aim to the left of a redbrick farm workshop and proceed beneath the electricity wires to go over a stile and walk through the farm complex and along the farm drive to arrive at the **B4439** road. Go right and in 100m you arrive at the car park of the Navigation Inn where you can enjoy refreshments.

If you wish to visit the Kingswood Lock Gates, continue down to the canal bridge and walk the towpath going southeast until you reach a junction of canals. This is a link canal that leads to the Stratford-upon-Avon Canal – detailed directions are recorded at the end of this chapter.

Longer Walk

Continue by walking to the left of the magnificent National Trust Manor Hall (nearby is Packington Hall, another attractive National Trust property). Bear left along a path via a kissing gate into **Baddesley Clinton churchyard** (it is a blaze of yellow daffodils in the spring) and then go right through a gate onto a path which leads over fields going in a general southwest/south direction. The clear way path arcs gently to the left as you go over a stile and passes through several gates to proceed to the right of **Lyons Farm** onto a lane.

Go left along the lane for about 450m, passing by the superb converted **Rowington Mill**, then go right through a gate into pastureland. The path starts in a southeast direction passing Quarry Farm (to the left) then bends right to a stile to continue in a southwest direction over three more fields and stiles to arrive in the churchyard at Rowington.

Exit the churchyard via the front gate and leave the Heart of England Way. Cross over the B4439 road and go right along the pavement through the village of **Rowington**. In just over 100m bear left to walk down **Mill Lane** and to stroll past attractive private residences for some 400m. Now bear left again and take Badger Lane. Just before the entrance to Field Cottage go left over a stile and enjoy the pleasant view of colourful narrowboats on the Grand Union Canal below. Descend by the field hedge to the right and go over a stile at its corner, taking care as you pass through the grounds of a small farmhouse to reach a final stile onto the road outside the Tom o' the Wood Inn.

Now go left to cross **Turner's Green Bridge** over the Grand Union Canal, then go left again to descend onto the towpath of the canal. Proceed under the bridge and walk north along the attractive towpath for just over ½ mile (1.1km). You pass beneath Weston Hall Bridge (bridge no 64).

To visit the Kingswood Lock Gates

At the junction of canals, proceed along the towpath of the 'link canal' between the Grand Union and the Stratford-on-Avon canals passing beneath the railway bridge to reach the Kingswood Junction on the

Stratford-on-Avon Canal. Here, bear right to continue on the left bank of the Stratford-on-Avon Canal going north to reach a flight of nine lockgates at Lapworth.

When you have reached the top lock gate (no 9) turn around and descend by the side of these amazing gates – each gate is spaced only a few metres from its neighbour and the afternoon view in the summer is a colourful spectacle of narrowboats working their way through the sequence of locks. Between each of these nine lock gates is a larger reservoir of water to permit the manoeuvring of the long narrowboats and they provide a sort of isthmus.

Colourful narrowboats near Kingswood Junction

Return to the Grand Union Canal via the link canal and then bear left to continue along the towpath of the Grand Union Canal until you reach Kingswood Bridge. Leave the canal here and ascend up to the B4439 road. The Navigation Inn is across the road on the right.

WALK 25 – Ludlow Castle Countryside Walk

After touring the street attractions of Ludlow this walk takes you through typical Shropshire countryside into parkland. A steep ascent into Mortimer Forest is followed by a descent to a fine viewpoint over Ludlow and finishes with an opportunity to visit the impressive Ludlow Castle.

Distance:	8 miles (12.8km)
Duration:	Allow 4 to 4½ hours
Refreshments:	Numerous eating places in Ludlow
Walk Start:	17 miles (27km) north of Leominster, Ludlow is best approached on the A49 road. Go left onto the B4361 road then left by the church to arrive near Whitecliffe Common
Car Parking:	Park in Whitecliffe Road on the edge of Whitecliffe Common (GR 506743)
Terrain:	Mainly easy walking but with a long climb into Mortimer Forest. Generally good underfoot but some of the forest paths may be muddy in wet weather
OS Map:	Explorer 203 – Ludlow, Tenbury Wells and Cleobury Mortimer

From the car park walk up Whitcliffe Road and at the road junction (by the Whitcliffe Common) pause to enjoy the exceptionally fine views over the town of Ludlow, its castle and Titterstone Clee Hill beyond.

Now take the path on the common next to the road and then veer right on one of the many paths that lead down to Dinham Bridge over the **River Teme** – another nice view and viewing place where Ludlow Castle stands proudly above the far bank and children playing in the water by the weir add to a fine bridge scene.

Proceed over the bridge and ascend the narrow lane bearing gently left to arrive in Castle Square – where a visit into **Ludlow Castle** can be made. Continue into Market Street bearing left past the Buttercross and

Broad Street (seemingly full of half-timbered houses) into King Street and on to reach Bull Street. Go left along Bull Street to admire the superb Feathers Hotel – built in 1619 this old posting house is a remarkable example of the wood carver's skill.

Ludlow is a beautiful Shropshire town dominated by a superb and impressive red-stone castle. Built in the 11th century to keep out marauding Welsh raiders, it was later extended and finally abandoned in the 18th century. Today the castle is open to the public and there is a terraced walk around the castle to enjoy. The town itself was built by medieval stonemasons and there are many half-timbered buildings to admire including the Feathers Hotel, Castle Lodge, the Readers House and much of Old Street. St Laurence's Parish Church is the largest in Shropshire being 203ft/62m long and with a 135ft/41m tower. A fascinating town with much to see.

Retrace your steps into King Street keeping to the right pavement past Buttercross and go right into College Street. If you can spare time visit the impressive Church of St Lawrence. Continue down College Street, bearing left at its end and then right to descend steps to take a lane called Linney. The lane leads past some delightful large residences which back onto Linney Riverside Park. After 300m the lane bends sharp right but you continue ahead onto a footpath. This path leads over a couple of footbridges and then proceeds across pastureland to go through a kissing gate onto the pavement of Coronation Avenue (the B4361 road). Go left and in 90m go left again into Burway Lane.

Take Burway Lane past a series of attractive large houses. Just after passing the last house the lane becomes a farm track/drive and you proceed into the countryside. By the drive (on the left) to **Burway Farm** you see your first Shropshire Way waymarker and you follow these for the next mile. The track passes to the left of a further farm and after going through a gate you walk to the right of a hedge with the Bromfield road to the far right. The track arcs right to reach the road but do not go out of the field. Instead, go left and take a clear wide track inside the roadside hedge. To your left is an abundance of wild flowers and fine views of the hills beyond – seemingly environmentally friendly on the left and somewhat noisy dirty traffic on the right.

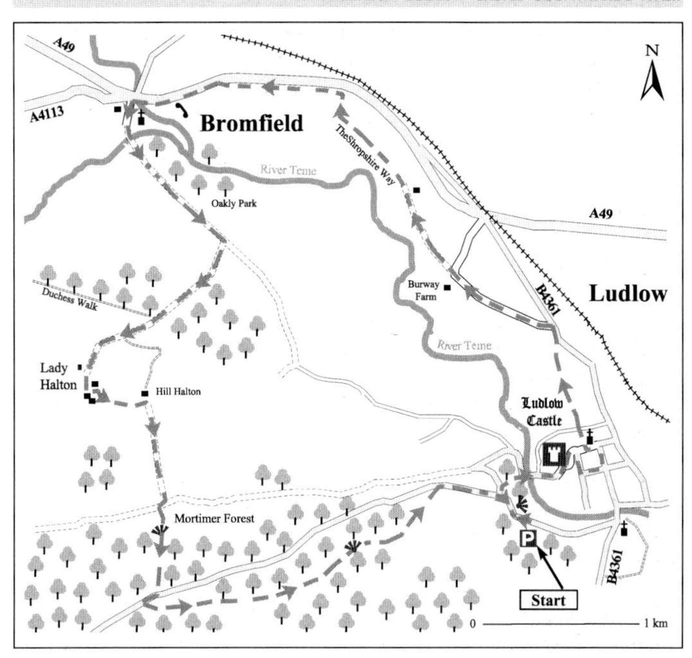

Follow the track going generally west for some 900m and you emerge onto the roadside pavement to continue past the Cookhouse cafe and restaurant. Some 150m beyond the cafe, and after crossing the bridge over the River Teme, go left into a peaceful lane. On the right is Bromfield Manor while on the left you can visit the **Church of St Mary the Virgin**.

A church was built on the confluence of the Rivers Teme and Onny as long ago as AD 900 and a church and Religious House stood here during the reign of Edward the Confessor (1042–66). Mentioned in Domesday Book of William the Conqueror (1080) it was in 1135 when the College of Secular Canons was transformed into a Priory of Regulars. Much of the church has been rebuilt over the years but parts of the Priory, which consisted of a quadrangle of buildings situated adjacent to the church, remain today. A very peaceful place to pause and the fine old Priory gatehouse has been renovated by English Heritage and the Landmark Trust.

Return to the lane and now walk south pausing at the fine bridge over the river. Continue along the tarmac lane (a bridleway) perhaps taking the nicely trimmed grass verge. Keep to the right at the entrance lodge to **Oakly Park** – a fine stretch of walking which takes you through delightful parkland.

About ½ mile/1km beyond the bridge, go right (southwest) to take a tarmac farm drive passing by conifers and oak trees in **Duchess Walk**. Ascending past the private driveway to Hill Halton you soon arrive in the farm complex of **Lady Halton**. Go left between the farm buildings and proceed through a new house gate. Veer right past farm barns and go through a farm gate and then left to take a half-built rough farm track (east direction). The track leads up to reach the rather nice half-timbered **Hill Halton**. Now go right (south) through a bridle gate to take a clear fenced track which soon starts to ascend. A further bridle gate leads into a hedged track that ascends to a lane.

Go right along the lane for 75m then go left through a further bridle gate onto a beautiful ascending path. The ascent becomes fairly steep so pause from time to time to enjoy the superb retrospective view which embraces Brown Clee Hill and Titterstone Clee Hill – the view gets better the higher you go.

You enter **Mortimer Forest** and continue the ascent through the trees – there are still glimpses of that improving view behind you. After crossing a forest track and a further ascent through forest you reach a forest lane. Here, go right for 90m then go left onto a clear pathway by the Mary Knoll House.

Pass to the left of the house, proceeding east past some farm buildings and soon you re-enter Mortimer Forest over a stile and onto a pleasant hedged walking track. When you reach a farm gate bear left to continue on a delightful hedged path which soon reaches open ground. The path becomes a lovely track with wild flowers in abundance (so many foxgloves) and with fine views over the hill to the north – a delightful stretch of walking. The track descends gently to a junction of forest tracks. Cross over and continue on the path opposite into the forest, now following yellow marker posts until you reach a path inside the forest edge.

Go left and take this path, always keeping by the edge of the forest, and you reach a forest lane. Go right down this quiet lane and in 450m you reach the lane junction by a viewing point over Ludlow. Bear right and the car park in some 250m.

Some of the many half-timbered buildings in Ludlow

WALK 26 – Brown Clee Hill Walk

A fine hill walk past the old fort at Nordy Bank and up to the trig point on Brown Clee Hill (1772ft/540m). The descent is a truly peaceful delight.

Distance:	7½ miles (12km)
Duration:	Allow 4 hours
Refreshments:	There are no pubs/inns along the walk
Walk Start:	Clee Hill is about 6 miles (9.5km) west of Cleobury Mortimer. From the A4117 Cleobury Mortimer–Ludlow road proceed up the B4364 road and through the village of Stoke St Milborough. Start from the car park about ¾ mile (1.2km) north of Stoke St Milborough
Car Parking:	There is a small car park just off the Stoke Bank Lane (GR 568834)
Terrain:	Hilly walking on generally good footpaths
OS Map:	Explorer 203 – Ludlow

From the car park go through the hand-gate onto Brown Clee Common and walk northeast on the clear green path/track which is close to the hedge on the right. Maintain the general line passing a lower path to the left and soon you see some sheep pens. Walk to the left of the pens after which the path arcs gently left. Ahead there is a fine view of the communication aerial on the top of Brown Clee Hill and to the left the remains of **Nordy Bank Fort** can be clearly seen. As the delightful path arcs left near to the old fort you join an asphalt track to go through gates onto a lane near to a further parking area.

Go right and take this quiet lane which leads into the hamlet of Cockshutford. By the telephone box in **Cockshutford**, go left and descend a narrow lane. In about 100m go right over a footbridge into pastureland. Aim generally north for a mid-field hedge gap, then walk by the left field hedge. At a small copse go left over a stile and proceed to the right of farm buildings to a mid-field farm gate. Continue through a second farm gate and onto a hedged track which emerges via a further gate onto a lane in **Abdon**.

Go right past the old manor house and where the lane bends sharp left continue ahead in front of a cottage with a red door. Proceed ahead up the drive to Manor Park Cottage. The path passes in front of the cottage then bears left over a small footbridge to reach a stile in the top left-hand corner of the garden. Proceed over this stile and take the footpath going generally northwest over several stiles. Go through a gateway onto a lane and go right past a telephone box to ascend the lane past **Bank House**. After passing the entrance drive to Dingle Cottage (on the left), go left over a stile and take the clear track (bridleway) ahead – you are now on the Shropshire Way with its 'buzzard' waymarkers. The track ascends sharply for about ¾ mile/1.2km going generally southeast.

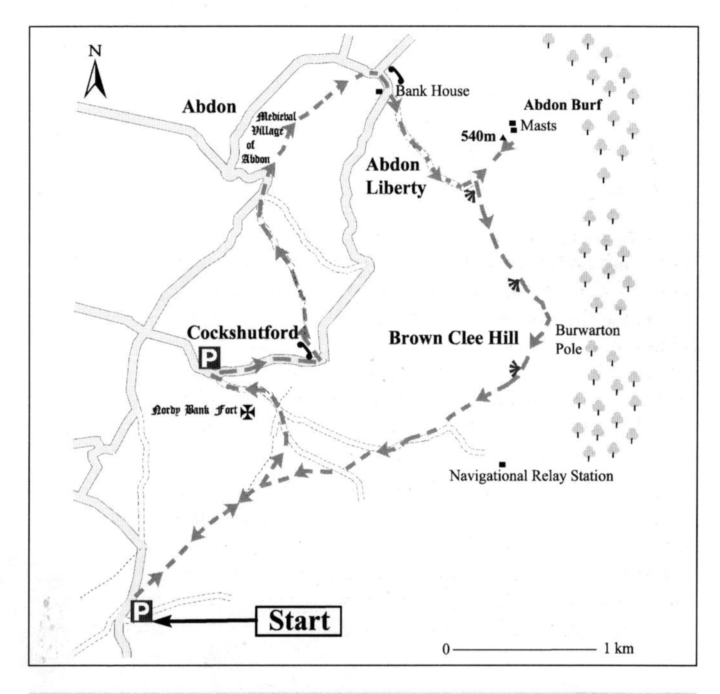

At the top of the track you reach a path going right but ahead is **Abdon Burf** (1772ft/540m) which will attract you. Continue ahead ascending to the trig point in front of the communication masts. Here spare time to recover your breath and to admire the hill scene.

Picturesque cottage in Abdon

Retrace your steps to the path and bear left to follow the ridge top of **Brown Clee Hill**. As you descend gently towards the trees near **Burwarton Pole** you will enjoy a superb valley view to your right.

Proceed through the gate near to the trees and continue right until you reach a footpath going right (south/southwest) which descends the valley of Clee Hill as you leave the Shropshire Way waymarkers behind. Descend the attractive easy path which contours the hill about halfway down the hillside. This is a peaceful descent where sheep are the only company and occasionally you cause the flutter of bird wings as they rise from the fern growth. Maintain a general southwest direction and in about 1½ miles/2.5km you pass to the right of the sheep pens you passed on the way up the hill.

Rejoin the pathway you started on, veering towards the left hedge and in about ¾ mile/1.2km you arrive back at the car park.

Walk 27 – Bewdley and the Wyre Forest

A walk by the River Severn followed by a stroll through the delightful Wyre Forest to enjoy one of the largest areas of semi-natural woodland in the UK. To conclude there is the opportunity to meander the attractive town of Bewdley.

Distance:	6 miles (9.6km)
Duration:	Allow 3 to 3½ hours
Refreshments:	Tea rooms and pubs in Bewdley
Walk Start:	Bewdley is 4 miles (6.5km) west of Kidderminster on the A456 road. Bear left onto the B4190 road to enter the town then go left immediately after the bridge over the River Severn to the car park
Car Parking:	Pay and display car park in Gardness Meadow by the River Severn (GR 789751)
Terrain:	Mainly level walking but with a couple of undulations. Generally good underfoot but could be muddy on the woodland paths
OS Map:	Explorer 218 – Wyre Forest and Kidderminster

From the Gardness Meadow car park walk along the pavement above the **River Severn** towards the bridge. Cross over the main road and continue along the riverside path going generally northwest. The River Severn is a major fishing river and you are likely to see fishermen on the banks and in the river in waders. After leaving behind the town you walk in attractive countryside with some parkland and picnic tables – there are a couple of stiles to negotiate.

After about 1 mile/2km of pleasant riverside walking you see the stanchions of the former railway bridge. Here, go left (west) on a wider path with a stream on your right. This leads to a stile and you cross over the stream to follow its right bank. The path becomes a track as it meanders by the stream. You pass by Liebmoon Boxer Kennels and then the Worcestershire **Nature Conservation Trust area** of Knowles Coppice

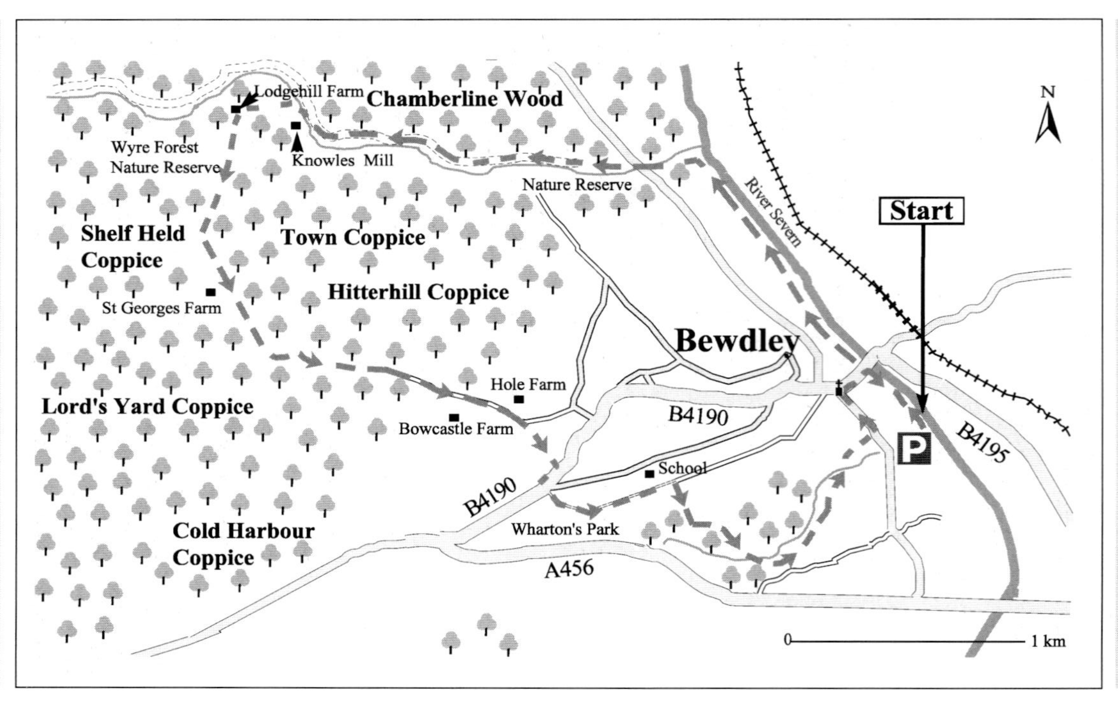

N
Start
Lodgehill Farm
Chamberline Wood
Wyre Forest
Nature Reserve
Knowles Mill
Nature Reserve
River Severn
Shelf Held
Coppice
Town Coppice
Hitterhill Coppice
St Georges Farm
Bewdley
Hole Farm
Lord's Yard Coppice
Bowcastle Farm
B4190
B4195
P
School
B4190
Wharton's Park
Cold Harbour
Coppice
A456
0
1 km

Reserve and reach a footbridge to **Knowles Mill** (National Trust) and a cottage. The cottage carries a delightful verse:

The dawn of the morn for glory
The hush of the night for peace
In the garden at eve says the story
God walks and his smile brings release.

Proceed right around the back of the mill building and go over a stile onto a lovely path which ascends into covered oak woodland. The clear path soon arcs left descending to go over a stile below **Lodgehill Farm**. Ascend the hill slope to a further stile set to the left of the farm and continue through the beautiful **Wyre Forest Nature Reserve** area where wild flowers abound and green woodpeckers may be seen in the trees. Proceed over a dismantled railway line and continue in a southwest direction on a clear path through the trees.

About 600m from Lodgehill Farm you meet a junction of paths where go left (southeast) and you soon reach an open area to the left of **St George's Farm**. After a further 600m the clear woodland path arcs left (west-southwest) and follows the line of a farm drive until you reach and go over a stile as you exit the woodland at Coppice Gate. Maintain the same walking line on the lane as it passes the entrance to **Bowcastle Farm** (on the right) and then, at the drive on the left to **Hole Farm**, go right over a footbridge onto pastureland.

The path soon becomes a hedged path and you emerge onto a tarmac drive as you enter a residential caravan site. Follow the waymarkers. As you ascend between the large caravans look out for a fire hydrant and electrical box. Here go right and then left by the side of the first caravan and take a hedged path to reach the B4190 road. Go right to a road junction. At the junction cross over the road with care and take a lane between houses until you reach open common ground known as **Wharton's Park** with a golf course visible over the valley.

Once clear of the houses go left and take a clear path at the back of a row of houses. This leads past a **school** with its sports ground to the right. At the end of the sports area, go right into Park Dingle. At the junction of paths proceed ahead slightly left and take the path above Snuffmill Dingle. After about 300m bear right and descend (a rather steep descent) through the trees and go over a footbridge. Climb the

The High Street, Bewdley

steep steps and go over a stile near to a lane. Follow the waymark direction aiming for a stile on the far left corner. This is a pleasant short hill walk with a nice view over Bewdley.

Continue through a gate by Snuffmill Pools (an entrance for fishermen) and take the path to the right of the fence. This leads into a hedged path on the entrance to Bewdley and you arrive in the High Street. Go left but do spare time to look at some of the old houses in the High Street, then go right into Load Street.

Bewdley High Street *– note the Baptist Church built in 1649 which faces the Methodist Church (1795). The Redhorne was built by the Prattinton family in 1765. At the approach to Load Street note the Bailiff's House (1610) – this fine example of elaborate timber framing was built by Thomas Bolston.*

Load Street *– The present St Anne's Church was built in 1745–48 by Thomas Woodward of Chipping Campden. It replaced a 16th-century timber church which included a medieval guild and chantry chapels.*

The George Hotel *is one of the fine timber-framed buildings in Load Street. It was a coaching inn and during the 19th century coaches ran to Birmingham, Worcester, Bristol and London. Telford's Bridge was designed by Thomas Telford for £11,000 in 1798.*

Meander Load Street until you reach the beautiful bridge. At the bridge go right and take the riverside pavement back to Gardness Meadow car park.

Walk 28 – Lickey Hills and Waseley Country Park

A fine walk over cattle-grazed hills for panoramic views over Birmingham and the Heart of England landscape.

Distance:	5 miles (8km)
Duration:	Allow 2½ to 3 hours
Walk Start:	Lickey is some 4 miles (6.5km) northeast of Bromsgrove. Take the A38 road and at the road island in Lickey End continue on the B4096 towards Lickey. Just before Lickey, go left onto a lane leading to Beacon Hill
Car Parking:	Free car parking at Beacon Hill (GR 987758)
Terrain:	Undulating. Generally good underfoot but there could be muddy areas in wet weather
OS Map:	Explorer 219 – Wolverhampton and Dudley

From the car park walk up to the tower on the rise of **Beacon Hill** for a fine view across the metropolis of Birmingham. (The tower was erected to commemorate the gift of the hills to the city of Birmingham in 1907 by Edward George Jar and Henry Cadbury for the use of the people of Birmingham for leisure, health and recreation.) Continue over the hill then descend to the left to meet the North Worcestershire Path. Bear left and take the clear path descending through trees following the fircone waymark and with the **golf course** to the right. The path veers north and runs to the right of a lane until it emerges onto the lane. Cross over the lane and continue over a stile along the North Worcestershire Path on a clear track heading northwest. After going through a gate the track widens and there are pleasing views over Birmingham to the right.

After about 400m the track arrives at a road. Bear left along the road to cross the bridge over the **A38** road. Walk past several houses then bear left to enter Redhill Lane. Continue on the North Worcestershire Way as it veers to the right into Waseley Hill Country Park and ascends via a stile and then a kissing gate onto a delightful hill-top path going

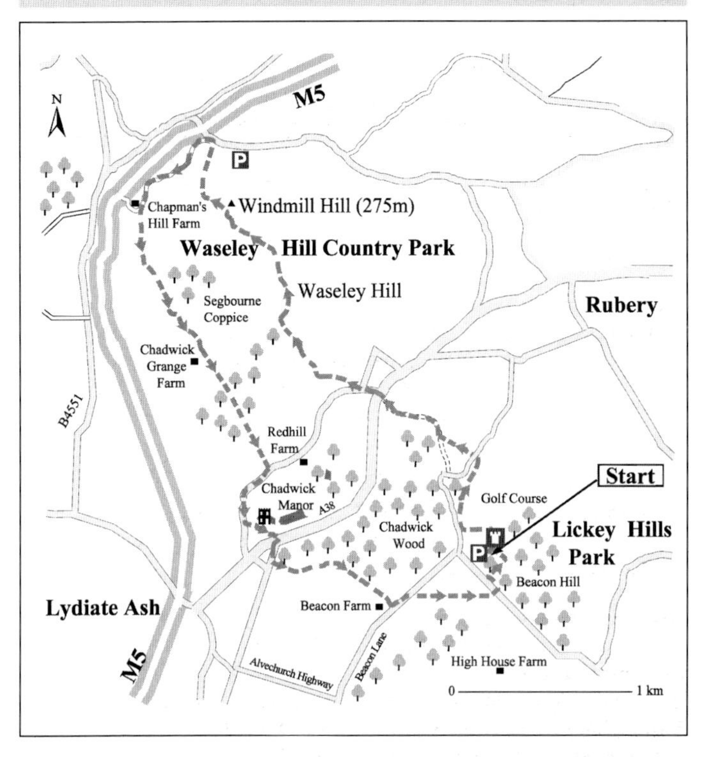

generally north. There are superb views all round – do pause from time to time to enjoy the fine retrospective view over Rubery and the Lickey Hills. As you progress up **Waseley Hill** you will enjoy **Waseley Hill Country Park** and the view to the north from the A4 topograph (erected in 1978) on **Windmill Hill**.

On a clear day the view embraces the Malverns, the Black Mountains and Sugar Loaf in Wales, Bredon Hill, the Long Mynd, the Derbyshire Hills, Edge Hill and Broadway Hill – a truly superb hilltop view.

Continue by descending over stiles with a picnic and parking area to the right. The route bears left to reach a lane via a stile and then continues left along the lane which runs parallel with the M5 over the hill. After passing **Chapman's Hill Farm** (on the right) leave the North Worcestershire Path to continue on a stony bridleway going south/southeast. This hedged track descends away from the noisy M5 with the cars seeming to get smaller. It is a pleasing walk with lovely old sycamore and beech trees adding to the scene. You pass a pool of bulrushes below **Segbourne Coppice**. With Chadwick Grange Farm down a lane to the right, go over a stile into pastureland and aim southeast for woodland. Enter the wood of beech trees and in spring you will be charmed by a magnificent ground cover of bluebells – a delightful picture. Exit the wood over a stile and take the path to a kissing gate where there is a sign left to 'Rubery'.

Tower on the rise of Beacon Hill

Go through the kissing gate and bear right to cross over the concrete drive to **Chadwick Grange Farm** and proceed over a stile onto Redhill Lane. Go right and descend past some delightful cottages and Chadwick Manor Farm entrance on the right. About 300m from the stile, go left over a small bridge and walk between **Chadwick Manor** and its outbuildings to a further stile. Follow the waymark direction to another stile onto the A38 road. Here, go left for about 15m past a bus stop, then cross the A38 with great care to a gap in the central barrier of the dual carriageway. Proceed to a tarmac track on the other side of the A38 to reach a small car park area. In 100m go left up a bridleway by the side of Beaconwood and the Winsel Nature Reserve. This leads through the gardens of a beautiful house called Winsel Cottage to enter Beaconwood via a metal gate. Take the good footpath in the trees to the right of the somewhat muddy bridleway. The path arcs right and eventually emerges through **Beacon Farm** to arrive in Beacon Lane.

Go left up the lane for 100m then go right through a gate to take a clear path which diagonally crosses a large cultivated field. The route goes east over three more stiles until you reach Monument Lane. Cross over the lane and enter the woodland, go left and then right to take a clear path which meets a stone path coming from the right. Now go left through a hedge gap and you see the **Beacon Hill** tower and can return to the car park.

WALK 29 – Kenilworth Castle and Honiley

An easy but very pleasant walk in attractive Warwickshire countryside. You will visit a beautiful church at Honiley and have the opportunity to visit English Heritage's magnificent Kenilworth Castle.

Distance:	4 miles (6.4km) or 5½ miles (8.8km)
Duration:	Allow 3 hours
Refreshments:	The Queen and Castle pub by Castle Green, Kenilworth
Walk Start:	From the centre of Kenilworth take the B4013 road and follow the castle signs
Car Parking:	Free car park opposite Castle Green near Kenilworth Castle (GR 279724)
Terrain:	Easy walking on good paths, tracks and lanes
OS Map:	Explorer 221 – Coventry and Warwick

From the car park go west on a clear path by the side of the Kenilworth Castle walls and proceed over a stile by a gate near to a beautiful pink thatched cottage. Go right past the cottage and go over a stile onto a track. Now go left and in 125m leave the track by going right over a stile into a cultivated field and take the clear path going diagonally northwest across the field. Maintain this general line over four fields and several stiles. You see Pleasance Farm on the left and will emerge on **Chase Lane** by a red-brick terraced row.

Go left and along the lane for about 1 mile (1.4km) passing by the Pleasance and to the right of **Chase Wood**. As you approach the end of the wood, the large complex of **Warriors Lodge Farm** will be close. At the wood end, go left and descend the stony farm track to the west of Chase Wood. In some 400m you reach a junction of footpaths. Here you can decide whether you wish to visit Honiley.

Shorter walk

If you are content with the shorter walk, go left here and walk the clear, straight track to the right of a hedge with Chase Wood further to the left – as described under 'Final part of the walks', below.

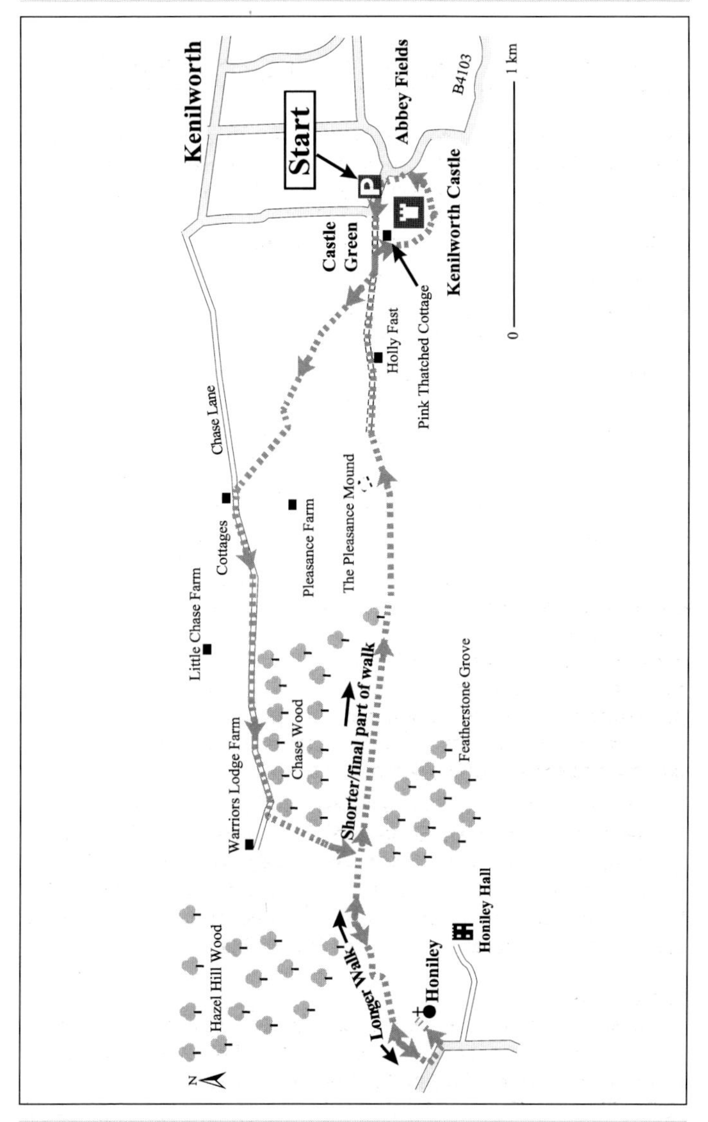
Kenilworth
Start
Abbey Fields
B4103
1 km
0
Castle Green
Kenilworth Castle
Pink Thatched Cottage
Holly Fast
Chase Lane
Cottages
Pleasance Farm
The Pleasance Mound
Little Chase Farm
Chase Wood
Shorter/final part of walk
Featherstone Grove
Warriors Lodge Farm
Hazel Hill Wood
Longer Walk
Honiley
Honiley Hall
N

Longer walk

To go to Honiley, go right and follow the field hedge to the field corner where go over a footbridge and ascend west-southwest to the right of field hedges. Go over the stile at the top of the field and go left over two further stiles to reach a road. Go left along the quiet road for about 70m, then go left again to pass by the Malt-house and to arrive at **Honiley Church**.

St John the Baptist Church was built in 1723 although there is evidence of it being a much earlier place of worship. It is believed that Sir Christopher Wren drew the design for the church when dining with John Sanders. The church has a superb baroque-style west tower topped by an octagonal spire with a ball and weathercock on the apex. Today there are six bells in the tower

Kenilworth Castle (English Heritage)

although the sixth (the treble) was only added in 1977 in celebration of the Jubilee of Queen Elizabeth II. The gate piers leading into the churchyard were carved with an elephant heads motif which is the insignia of John Sanders who lived in nearby Honiley House. The elephant motif is repeated on the front pew in the church.

Retrace your steps to the junction of paths and now proceed ahead (east) on a wide green track to the right of a hedge with Chase Wood further to the left.

Final part of walks

Walk this straight track for the next ½ mile/1km, where you go over a stile/footbridge. Continue ahead and Kenilworth Castle will come into view. After crossing the **Pleasance Mound** you go over a stile to take a hedged footpath which leads to the farm drive to **Holly Fast**.

As you continue up the farm drive you are rewarded with a superb view of the castle which is fast approaching. Just before reaching the pink thatched cottage, go right over a stile to take a signed footpath which circles around the castle walls and emerges by the car park. You can visit Kenilworth Castle after you have enjoyed refreshments.

The red sandstone walls of the magnificent Kenilworth Castle can be seen for many miles and are particularly colourful in the evening sunset. It was a stronghold for the Lords and Kings of England in the 11th and 12th centuries and was remodelled as a palace in the 14th century by John of Gaunt. The castle has a fascinating history to discover including the fact that it was the setting for much of the action in Sir Walter Scott's 'Kenilworth'. Today the castle and its fine Tudor gardens are owned and looked after by English Heritage.

Walk 30 – Braunston and the Grand Union and Oxford Canals

A pleasant stroll through historic Braunston village and then along the Grand Union and Oxford canals to see a medieval church set in the countryside.

Distance:	4 miles (6.4km)
Duration:	Allow 2 to 2½ hours
Refreshments:	Three pubs in Braunston: the Wheatsheaf, The Green (Tel. 01788 890748); the Admiral Nelson, Dark Lane; the Old Plough, High Street (Tel. 01788 890000)
Walk Start:	Braunston is 3 miles (4.8km) northwest of Daventry just off the A45 road
Car Parking:	Park with consideration on the wide High Street in Braunston (GR 541662)
Terrain:	Easy walking on canal towpaths and good footpaths
Map:	Explorer 222 – Rugby and Daventry, Southam and Lutterworth

From the post office in the High Street take the Ashby St Ledgers road going northeast. At the junction with the Barby and Welton roads (by the Green) proceed right into **Welton Road**. Within 20m cross over the road and follow the sign 'Quincy-Voisins' onto a footpath between houses. Descend the path (part of the Jurassic Way) through a couple of iron kissing gates onto common land with the tall chimney of the Pump House clearly visible ahead. Do not walk down to the canal but bear left to go through two further kissing gates to arrive at a road corner on Dark Lane.

Walk down **Dark Lane** into **Little Braunston** and you pass by a number of attractive houses. The lane draws close to the Grand Union Canal and you pass to the left of and past the **Admiral Nelson** pub onto a stone track. Proceed past the next lock gate and soon the track arcs to reach the Anchor House where you cross over the canal on bridge no

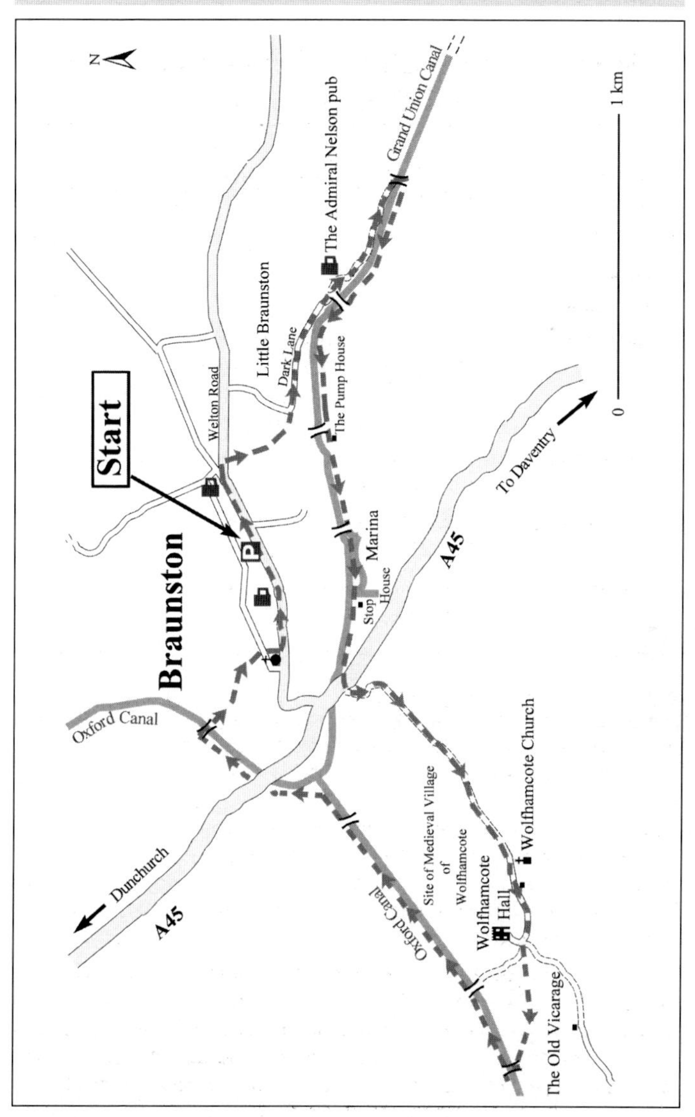
N
Start
Braunston
Welton Road
Little Braunston
Dark Lane
The Admiral Nelson pub
Grand Union Canal
The Pump House
Marina
Stop House
A45
To Daventry
0
1 km
Oxford Canal
Dunchurch
A45
Oxford Canal
Site of Medieval Village of Wolfhamcote
Wolfhamcote Church
Wolfhamcote Hall
The Old Vicarage

5 to arrive by Top Lock. Descend left to the towpath, perhaps visiting the Braunston Tunnel Gift Shop.

Continue by going beneath bridge no 5 and along the excellent towpath. This is a very busy stretch of canal and you are likely to see a number of colourful narrowboats negotiating the series of lock gates. You soon pass the Admiral Nelson now on the other side of the canal and can cross over bridge no 4 if you need refreshment.

The Admiral Nelson *was built in 1730 and is said to be haunted. Apparently a figure in black has the habit of walking through walls.*

Continue along the towpath and soon you pass Bottom Lock and the tall chimney of the **Pump House** (on the left).

The Pump House *has a tall red-brick chimney with the letters G. U. C. (Grand Union Canal) and the date 1897 in blue bricks. The Pump House contained a steam engine to pump water from the small reservoirs to the high levels.*

Proceed along the towpath to see numerous narrowboats either moored on the canalside or in the huge **marina** area to the left. Continue to **Stop House**.

Stop House *is a former tollhouse where boats travelling on the Grand Union and Oxford canals paid money for using the canals. Today the building has been converted into an information and exhibition room with a series of displays revealing the origin of the canals during the Industrial Revolution and their later demise from major transports of commercial goods when the Great Central Line railway opened a station in Braunston in 1899.*

Before continuing along the towpath look up towards the village of Braunston. The large Greek-style building is called Berryfields.

Berryfields *was the Braunston rectory which was built by the Rev A B Clough to 'accommodate his bride in the manner to which she had become accustomed'. His bride was the daughter of a Mr R Howson Lamb who owned the nearby Bragborough Hall.*

Leave the towpath at bridge no 91 ascending to the left of the bridge up to the busy A45 road. Cross over the A45 with care and take the footpath opposite signed 'Wolfhamcote Church'. Proceed along the

Medieval re-enactment at Warwick Castle (Walk 32)

Coughton Court (National Trust) (Walk 34)

Clopton Bridge from the Royal Shakespeare Theatre, Stratford (Walk 38)

Braunston Marina

wide stone concrete strip track which soon arcs right. In about 800m you reach **Wolfhamcote Church**.

> ***Wolfhamcote*** *was originally a small village which was affected by the plague and the church is all that remains. The remains of the old medieval village are barely visible. Admission to the church is by acquiring the key from the neighbouring cottage or the Old Vicarage. Today the church comes to life on Christmas Day for its only service of the year but cushions and hot water bottles may be essential.*

Continue along the track passing to the left of **Wolfhamcote Hall** to go through a gateway and cross a bridge over the now dismantled Great Central Line railway. You soon reach the Oxford Canal at bridge no 98. Cross over the bridge and descend to the towpath of the **Oxford Canal**. Proceed northeast towards Braunston. This is a very pleasant towpath walk with narrowboats moored at the canalside and with the view of Braunston ahead.

After passing beneath a 'turnover' bridge (it has two ramps to enable towing horses to cross to the towpath on the opposite bank without unhitching the towrope), you arrive at the junction with the Grand Union Canal. Two fine iron bridges greet you – twin bridges built at Horseley Iron Works in the Black Country.

Bear left to continue on the Oxford Canal towpath, passing beneath the A45 (London Road) Bridge. Leave the towpath at the next canal bridge. Cross over the bridge and a stile to walk by the left hedge of pastureland with the impressive spire of All Saints Church ahead.

At the field end bear left over a further stile and ascend the path to a final stile onto Church Road in Braunston. Cross over the road and enter the churchyard of **All Saints Church** (built in 1849). Exit the churchyard into High Street where go left to get back to your car.

*The name **Braunston** derives from Brandseton – Brant or Brand's 'ton' (or village). The name first appeared in AD 956 on a Royal Charter when the land was granted to a nobleman. Brant (Brand) is the name of the king's Anglo-Saxon Lord.*

At the time of the plague, which decimated nearby Wolfhamcote, the small village of Braunston was isolated from the outside world and in this way avoided the effects of the plague The arrival of the canal system towards the end of the 18th century caused the village to expand to look after the canal workforce. Blacksmiths, carpenters, ropemakers and saddlers arrived and at one stage there were no less than 12 inns. Today Braunston is an unpretentious village with but three inns but the names of some of the old buildings remind us of a bygone period – the Old Plough, the Village Bakery, Ye Olde Harrow, the Wheatsheaf.

WALK 31 – Henley-in-Arden and the Mount

After a stroll along the High Street of the picturesque Tudor town of Henley-in-Arden there is a short hill ascent to enjoy the superb views from the top of Beaudesert Mount before you progress into gentle rolling Warwickshire countryside. A descent to stroll the towpath of the Stratford-upon-Avon Canal leads to a meander along the banks of the River Alne as you return to historic Henley-in-Arden.

Distance:	5¼ miles (8.4km)
Duration:	Allow 3 hours
Refreshments:	The White Swan Hotel, High Street, Henley-in-Arden
Walk Start:	Henley-in-Arden is 8 miles (13km) north of Stratford-upon-Avon on the A3400 road. At the traffic lights take the B4189 road towards Warwick following the parking sign that leads to the Prince Henry car park at the back of the High Street in Henley-in-Arden.
Car Parking:	There is free parking in the Prince Henry car park (GR 152658)
Terrain:	One short hill to climb but generally easy walking on good footpaths
OS Map:	Explorer 220 – Birmingham

Exit the car park via Stylers Way to reach the High Street in the town before starting your walk take time to meander the colourful High Street in Henley-in-Arden. This Britain in Bloom winner offers floral beauty in the summer months and provides plenty of photo opportunities.

The White Swan Hotel was built about 450 years ago to replace an earlier inn which dated from 1352. It became a popular coaching inn in the mid 19th century being set on a Birmingham to London route and then until 1903 was the home of the local court. Samuel Johnson stayed at the inn and is believed to have written one of his books here. One of the upstairs rooms is said to be haunted by an 18-year-old girl called Virginia Black who died

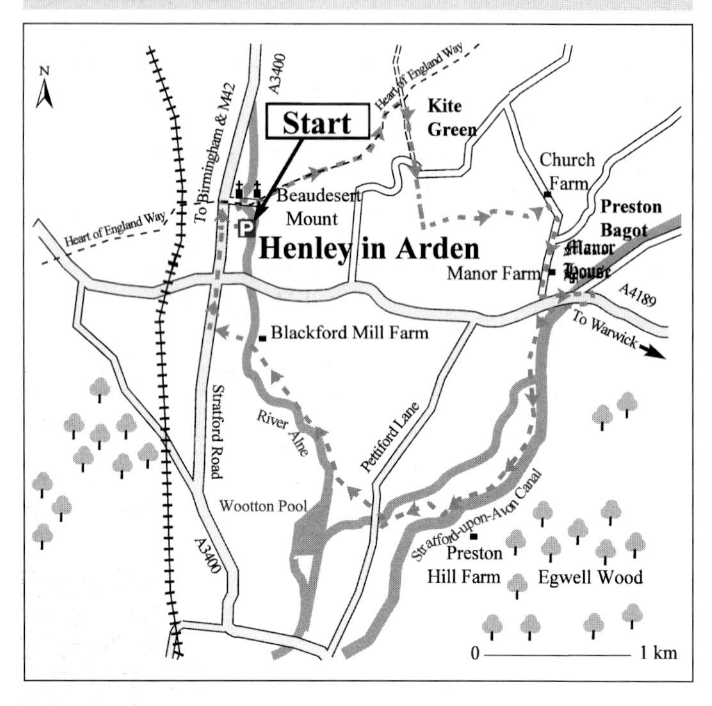

in the inn after falling down the staircase after a row with her lover. Today the inn is a regular watering hole for local walkers.

Go right from Stylers Way to start the walk from the timber-framed Guildhall and Church in the High Street and take Beaudesert Lane over the River Alne to reach Beaudesert Church. At the end of the churchyard proceed through a metal gate and follow the Heart of England Way waymarkers as you commence a steep but short ascent onto the top of **Beaudesert Mount**. From here you enjoy fine views over the town and surrounding countryside. Proceed in a northeast direction on the clear path over the old earthworks of the former castle of the de Montforts, ascending to reach a pair of stiles in the far field corner. Here, follow the Heart of England Way waymarkers and go over a stile to continue to the left of a hedge. In about 200m go right over a stile and diagonally cross the next field to go over a further stile and go right down Edge Lane for about 400m until you reach the road in **Kite Green**. Go left along the quiet lane and where it lane bends sharp left, continue ahead (at the public footpath sign) to go through a metal gate on the left. and proceed up a tarmac drive.

Go over the stile to the right of the next gate and follow a narrow hedged path. You pass by a house on your left and a metal fence as you continue into the next field. About halfway over this field go left and aim for a mid-hedge stile. Go over this stile and maintain your east line as you walk to the left edge of several fields and go over several stiles aiming towards the buildings of **Church Farm** which appears directly ahead. Proceed to the gate set to the right of the farm buildings.

Go through the gate onto a lane. Now go right and walk down the lane, passing by **Manor Farm** on your left before you reach the B4189 Henley to Warwick road. Go left along the road for about 200m where you see the attractive russet-coloured, half-timbered, 16th-century **Preston Bagot Manor House**. Cross over the B4189, just after the Warwick Road Bridge, and now descend to the towpath of the

Preston Bagot Manor House

Stratford-upon-Avon Canal via a gate. Proceed southwest along the canal towpath for the next 1¼ miles (2km). This pleasant stretch of towpath walking continues until you reach the second canal bridge with **Preston Hill Farm** on your left. Cross over the bridge and take the tarmac track/lane opposite. In 175m this bends sharp left and soon you arrive at a road near the Pettiford Bridge. Go right over the bridge and in some 45m go left over a stile into pastureland. Bear right to diagonally cross the field and to go over a stile in its far left corner to meet the River Alne.

Take the riverside path going generally northwest with **Blackford Mill Farm** prominent ahead. You go over a couple of footbridges before reaching a division of paths. Here, bear left to stay fairly near to the river and to go through a gate set to the far left of the farm complex. Cross the footbridge over the River Alne and take a narrow path ahead by a fence until you reach a stile. Go over the stile and cross the school playing fields to a final stile which leads onto the A3400 road. Go right on the pavement of the **A3400** road into Henley-in-Arden. Stroll up the lovely High Street, with its many floral displays draping the shops, but look out for the white Milestone Cottage on your right. It has a milestone on the wall declaring 'From London CII miles' and it is immediately after this building that you go right into the archway entrance of Stylers Way to return to your car.

WALK 32 – Warwick Castle and the Grand Union Canal

An easy walk from Warwick Racecourse that meanders along the towpath of the Grand Union Canal and by the side of the picturesque River Avon before arriving near the magnificent Warwick Castle and then returning to the racecourse. There is an opportunity to visit the superb castle.

Distance:	5 miles (8km)
Duration:	Allow 2½ to 3 hours' walking (overall 4 to 5 hours)
Refreshments:	Many pubs and tea rooms in the much visited town of Warwick
Car Parking:	Park by the roadside in Friars Street, Warwick, or on race days in Warwick Racecourse car park off Friars Street, Warwick (GR 277647)
Terrain:	Easy walking on canal towpaths and good footpaths
OS Map:	Explorer 221 – Coventry and Warwick

Walk to the end of the car park – inside the Warwick Racecourse entrance. Now go left and cross over the course and walk to the left of the golf driving range building. Immediately past the building go right and take the wide green track going north. You walk between the **golf course** and the **driving range** and in about 300m you reach the racecourse once again. Cross over the course and proceed over the stile opposite onto a footpath by a small factory complex. Continue ahead until you reach the corner of common land by the railway line. Here bear left along the path with the hedge and railway line to your right. After about 500m go right over stiles to cross the railway line, then take a fenced path between factory buildings until you reach the **A425** road. Cross over the road with care and continue on the waymarked footpath opposite.

You are now following a footpath on the right of the Grand Union Canal for the next 500m until you reach a road. Go left at the road to

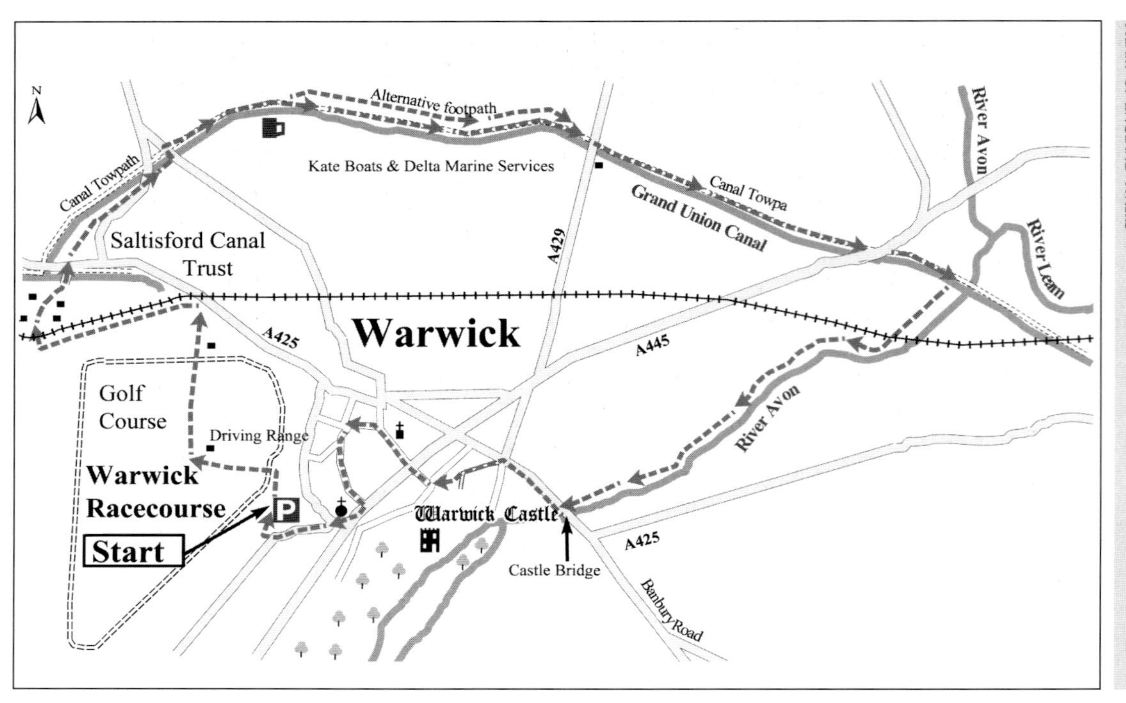
N
Alternative footpath
Kate Boats & Delta Marine Services
Canal Towpath
Canal Towpa
Grand Union Canal
River Avon
River Leam
Saltisford Canal Trust
A429
Warwick
A425
A445
Golf Course
Driving Range
River Avon
Warwick Racecourse
Start
Warwick Castle
A425
Castle Bridge
Banbury Road

cross over the canal and then go right and descend to the towpath on the other side of the canal. For the next 1½ miles/2.6km the walk takes you along the good towpath of a canal – in the spring it appears to be a breeding ground for ducks, coots and moorhens. At the first lock, the Cape of Good Hope pub may tempt you on the far bank. You pass Warwick Hospital (on the opposite bank) after which there are some attractive gardens backing on to the canal bank. A number of narrowboats add colour to the canal scene and there are always boats moored near to **Kate Boats** and **Delta Marine Services**.

After passing beneath bridge no 46 (just before the viaduct over the River Avon) look out for the metal steps descending to the left. Go down these steps to join the Waterside Walk, a riverside walk which goes from Leamington to Warwick. Go right under the viaduct bridge and commence about a 1 mile/1.4km walk along the bank of the **River Avon**. You pass to the rear of a new Tesco store and go beneath a railway bridge before walking at the rear of houses with satellite TV aerials. With glimpses of the busy river to your left you see much river traffic in the summer months. You reach a large leisure area and Warwick Castle comes into view. You pass through the Ash Flaver gardens as you reach Castle Bridge. Ascend the steps to reach the busy A452 road, which cross with great care.

Go left onto **Castle Bridge** and to your right you have a most magnificent view of Warwick Castle with a fine reflection in the River Avon. Proceed along the pavement back into the town of Warwick. Enter **Warwick Castle** grounds at the main entrance gate and proceed up to the main entrance.

No journey to the area is complete without a visit to the impressive ***Warwick Castle*** *– a building which compares favourably with any great fortress house in Europe. It has outstanding tall and elegant towers, is surrounded by a fine motte and bailey and has superb gardens laid out by Capability Brown – this is a gem of a castle. It was converted to a house in the 17th century and is one of the few medieval fortresses to be continuously inhabited – by the Earls of Warwick.*

Warwick Castle

Continue the walk by exiting the castle grounds via a wall gate into Castle Street, Warwick. Meander up the attractive half-timbered streets, pausing by Oken's House which now contains Warwick Doll Museum and from where there is a fine view of St Mary's Church ahead. Proceed up Castle Street to Jury Street. The tourist information centre is on the right-hand corner and you will be amazed at the number of antique shops. Continue up Church Street and enter **St Mary's Church**. You can climb to the top of the high church tower for a superb view over Warwick and its wonderful castle.

The church dominates the view up Church Street. Built in 1123, the Beauchamp chapel was completed in 1464 and contains the tomb of Richard Beauchamp, Earl of Warwick. A stroll through the churchyard will take you to a little passage known as TINKATANK and as you walk down the passage you will hear how it got its name.

The former County Goal (in use from 1778 to 1860 and now part of Shire Hall – the county offices) can be seen in Northgate Street. At the end of Northgate Street bear left to walk past the library in Barrack Street, then bear left to enter Market Place, passing around the fine Market Hall and exiting into the pedestrianised Swan Street.

At the end of Swan Street go right down the High Street at the bottom of which is the superb Lord Leycester Hotel.

This magnificent 14th-century timber-framed building was once the property and meeting place of the Guild of St George the Martyr, the Holy Trinity and St Mary. It was acquired by Lord Leycester in 1571 who converted it into a hospital (hostel) for a Master and Twelve Brethren. The beautiful original Guildhall remains and part of the building is now a Museum of the Queen's Own Huzzars.

Proceed beneath the archway of the buildings then go right into Bowling Green Street. In 50m go left into Friars Street and return to the Warwick Racecourse car park where you started.

WALK 33 – Hanbury Hall Stroll

A pleasant walk in 'Archers' country. The walk leads to the hilltop Hanbury Church (now a Grade 1 listed building) which has been used in several episodes of the famous radio programme and the Bull Inn is at Inkberrow, 5 miles (8km) southeast. The walk proceeds through typical Worcestershire countryside and offers the opportunity to visit the impressive Hanbury Hall (National Trust).

Distance:	4 miles (6.4km)
Duration:	Allow 2 to 2½ hours
Refreshments:	Tea shop at Hanbury Hall (entrance fee payable by non-members of the NT), the Jenny Ring Craft Centre and the Vernon Arms pub in Hanbury village at the junction of the B4090 and B4091 roads. Or drive to the Bull Inn in nearby Inkberrow
Walk Start:	The northern end of a wood which stands on Piper's Hill, ½ mile (0.8km) north of Hanbury village. From Bromsgrove go south on the A38 then take the B4091 for 4 miles (6.5km). From Droitwich go east along the B4090 (the Salt Way) for 4 miles (6.5km) and turn left through Hanbury for 1½ miles (2.5km). From Alcester take the B4090 west for 8½ miles (13.5km) and turn right through Hanbury village
Car Parking:	Free parking off the B4091 road at the north end of Piper's Hill Wood (GR 97653)
Terrain:	Generally easy walking on good footpaths and along the towpath of the Worcestershire and Birmingham Canal but with a couple of undulations. The paths in Piper's Hill Wood may by muddy in winter or during wet periods
OS Map:	Explorer 204 – Worcester and Droitwich Spa

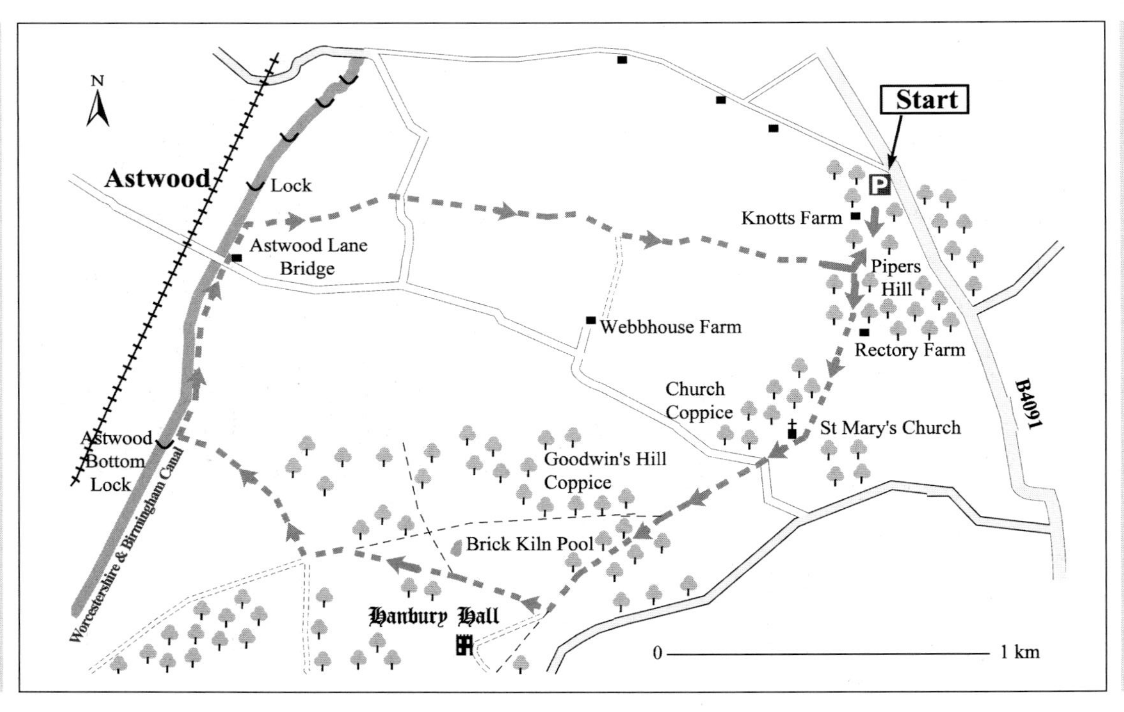
N
Start
P
Astwood
Lock
Knotts Farm
Astwood Lane Bridge
Pipers Hill
Webbhouse Farm
Rectory Farm
Church Coppice
St Mary's Church
B4091
Astwood Bottom Lock
Goodwin's Hill Coppice
Worcestershire & Birmingham Canal
Brick Kiln Pool
Hanbury Hall
0
1 km

From the car park at the top of Piper's Hill Wood descend south on a clear path to the right of a stone track to Knotts Farm. In about 200m bear left to join the main footpath which leads down to the stone track by a pool. Bear right at the track and take this past **Knotts Farm**. Continue through the woods keeping on the path as it hugs its right edge.

After leaving the wood bear slightly right to go through a kissing gate onto a path which leads through two further kissing gates to enter the churchyard of **St Mary's Church**, Hanbury. Initially arc left to walk the perimeter of the church and to enjoy the fine panoramic view which stretches to Bredon Hill, the Cotswold escarpment and the Malverns. Spare time to go into the attractive church.

St Mary's Church is sited on a hill-top (Hanbury is derived from the Saxons and means 'high town') where there was previously a Roman fort, later a Saxon monastery. St Mary's Church dates from AD 1210, being built in Bromsgrove sandstone in largely Georgian style. The fine church tower contains eight bells (one dating from 1678), which are renowned for their quality. The Vernon Chapel contains a number of fine marble monuments which record the history of the Vernon family of Hanbury Hall fame.

Continue the walk by going through the front gate to the church and descend the lane ahead. In about 70m veer right to go through a kissing gate into Hanbury Park (NT) and take the clear path going in a southwest direction for the next 800m. You go over a stile to enter a delightful avenue of oak trees and then fork left to pass a fenced area. Go over the stile onto a drive and continue on the same line past a pond. Just before a second pond go right and cross the drive once again. Pause here for a good view of **Hanbury Hall** and perhaps take the opportunity to visit the impressive 18th-century red-brick house.

Hanbury Hall was built in about 1700, possibly by Talman, the architect responsible for Chatsworth House, Derbyshire. The hall, a very fine example of the country house of that period, is now owned by the National Trust.

Continue from the drive by going over a stile into grassland following the direction of the waymark arrow to go over a further stile to the left of **Brick Kiln Pool**. Now go to the right of a small pool surrounded by large horse-chestnut trees aiming generally for a double stile in the far left-hand corner of Hanbury Park – take time to look left and see the rear view of the impressive hall. After going right over the second stile continue northwest on a clear path which leads over a footbridge and a further stile to arrive on the towpath of the Worcestershire and Birmingham Canal by **Astwood Bottom Lock**.

Hanbury Hall (National Trust)

Go right and follow the pleasant towpath for about 700m. You will probably hear the sound of fast trains on the line to your left. A colourful narrowboat is likely to pass by and will be very close to you. Fishermen may be competing for the roach, carp and other freshwater fish which are in the canal. About 125m after going beneath bridge no 40, go right over a stile to take a hedge path going generally east for just under 1 mile (1.9km). Initially you walk to the left of the hedge until you go over a stile onto a lane. Cross the lane and go over a stile to follow the right of the hedge as you continue over cultivated fields. There is a pleasant countryside view to the left where you are likely to see a number of horses (with their foals!). Some 200m after going over stiles and a farm track (ahead to your left you will see Piper's Hill Wood with Webbhouse Farm on the right), look out for a footbridge to the left. Cross the footbridge and now walk to the left of the hedge. As you go over a corner field stile you will see Knotts Farm in the far left corner of the next field, but maintain your line to reach and enter **Piper's Hill Wood** over a final stile.

About 20m into the wood, go left to join the main footpath and to pass **Knotts Farm** on a farm track. After passing the large pond bear left and take the waymarked footpath back into the woods. In about 150m bear right and you quickly arrive at the starting point.

WALK 34 – Alcester and the Coughton Court Walk

A pleasant countryside walk over typical Warwickshire farmland by the side of the meandering River Arrow with an opportunity to visit the impressive Coughton Court (National Trust).

Distance:	7 miles (11.2km)
Duration:	Allow 3 hours
Refreshments:	Several pubs and cafe shops in Alcester, the Throckmorton Arms in Coughton (GR 078070)
Walk Start:	Alcester is 8 miles (13km) west of Stratford-upon-Avon, just off the A46 road. Coughton is 2 miles (3km) northwest of Alcester
Car Parking:	Alcester town car park off School Road at the back of High Street (GR 088575)
Terrain:	Easy walking through pleasant Warwickshire countryside
OS Map:	Explorer 205 – Stratford-upon-Avon and Evesham

Alcester is a delightful small town which dates back to Roman occupation. A jumble of ancient roofs can be admired in Butter Street and there are fascinating friezes in Churchill House. Half-timbered buildings are dotted along the High Street and the renovated Malt Mill Lane is a delight to meander. The classical Town Hall was built in 1618 as a gift of Sir Fulke Greville and the superb building of St Nicholas Church dominates the High Street.

Depart the car park in Alcester and go right past the infant school to reach School Road. Go right to the junction where go left and proceed across the bridge over the **River Arrow**. Immediately before the Greig Hall Leisure Centre go left and take a clear track which soon descends left to continue by the side of the river through Alcester Playing Fields and in about 400m go left along an old dismantled railway line to go left across the bridge over the Arrow once again.

Just over the bridge go right along a footpath between the back of some new houses and the river. The path takes you through a small but pleasant park area by the river to reach a road. Go right along the pavement and cross the road just after crossing a further bridge over the Arrow. Now take a path between an office block and the river to go over a bridge stile and walk to the right of the Arrow over a series of cultivated fields and a stile. A pleasant ¾ mile stretch of easy riverside walking to reach and go over a stile onto the drive to Church Farm.

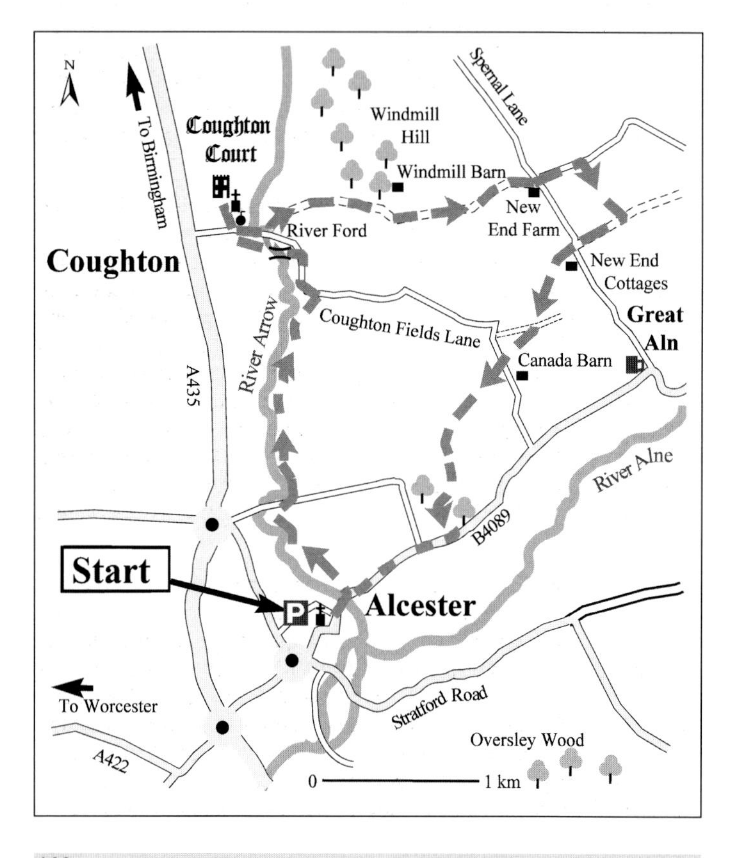

Go left to a lane and stroll an attractive country lane. Just after passing an old mill house go left (east) over a footbridge across the river to take a clear footpath over two fields, going through a kissing gate to reach a gate onto a lane sited immediately opposite the rear entrance to **Coughton Court** (NT). Walk to the front of this impressive manor house and take the opportunity to visit the fine building and attractive gardens.

Coughton Court has been the home of the Throckmorton family since 1409 and is one of the great Tudor houses. The present building is believed to date from 1530 being famous for its important associations with the Gunpowder Plot and the Civil War. It has a fine central gatehouse surrounded by a beautiful half-timbered courtyard which is best seen from the back of the building. There are formal gardens, two churches and a lovely short riverside walk to enjoy.

Return to the lane and go left to walk down to a popular ford over the River Arrow. Walk over the footbridge to the right of the **ford** and perhaps to count the ducks on the river. On the other side of the river cross the lane and bear left to go through a gate onto a stone farm track which follow for about 1 mile (1.4km). You pass **Windmill Hill Barn** to the left and eventually go through a metal gate onto Spernall Lane next to **New End Farm**. Go right for about 15m then cross the lane and proceed up the lane opposite the farm. Immediately after the last house on the right, go right down a clear path to follow the edge of a cultivated field and go over a stile onto a farm lane. Here, go right and take the farm lane back to Spernall Lane. You are now on the Heart of England Way and can follow the waymarkers back into Alcester.

Initially cross Spernall Lane and go over a stile a little to the left of the junction, then cross a small field to the right of a house. Go over a footbridge in the far corner of the field and quickly go left over a further stile, then go right and walk to the left of a hedge for about 800m. Pass through a gap in the hedge to walk on the other side of the hedge and follow the field to enter a narrow strip of trees. Cross over a track and go over a stile opposite with a small pond to the left, then descend southwest over pastureland to go over a further stile to the right of a large farm barn called **Canada Barn** to arrive in **Coughton Fields Lane**.

Cross the lane and proceed through the gate left opposite and then continue on a clear track to the right of a hedge soon ascending to a stile at the field end. Go over the stile and a further one in about 50m on the left. Go right and descend to go over a pair of stiles and an old bridge over the old dismantled railway line. In the next field go through a kissing gate next to the field gate and continue past a trig point (a massive 217ft/66m above sea level) and pause there for a fine view over Alcester and the surrounding countryside.

Town crier's championship, Alcester

Descend the field to go over a field stile, bearing left to follow the path through a narrow strip of trees to reach the **B4089** in Alcester. Go right and follow the pavement. You soon cross over the bridge once again and can then proceed up into Alcester to enjoy a most beautiful town – a proud winner of the national Britain in Bloom contest. When you have seen the sights it is possible to reach the car park at the back of the High Street by one of two narrow passageways to the right of the High Street.

Walk 35 – Abberley Hill Walk

A testing hill walk through superb Worcestershire countryside and passing the amazing Abberley Hall Tower. Nearby Witley Court is a fantastic place to visit.

Distance:	4½ miles (7.2km)
Duration:	Allow 2½ hours
Refreshments:	The Manor Arms pub in Abberley village
Walk Start:	Great Witley is 11½ miles (18.5km) northwest of Worcester on the A443 road
Car Parking:	Village hall car park at the junction of the B4197 in Great Witley (GR 758658)
Terrain:	Hilly (steep in parts) on generally good footpaths
OS Map:	Explorer 204 – Worcester and Droitwich Spa

From the car park cross over the A443 road with care and walk down the **B4197** Martley road. In about 100m go right up a house drive. Pass by a pond (on the left) and go over a stile at the drive end then follow the waymark direction over cultivated fields and three stiles to arrive at a lane over a fourth stile. Go right along the lane passing by the buildings of **Walsgrove Farm** (a goose farm?) After following the lane for some 900m you arrive at the **B4203** road. Here, go right along the roadside to the junction with the A443 road. Now go left and after following the road edge (with care) for 60m go left again (after the first house) to take a track at the back of houses and reach a stile by a gate.

Go over the stile and follow the waymarkers taking the clear main track through the trees. As the track arcs right you pass to the left of the buildings of **Abberley Hall** with a school sports fields to the left. At a junction of tracks, go right to join the Worcestershire Way going generally north-northeast. You pass close to the amazing Abberley **Clock Tower** which has a delightful chime. At the stone track end you will arrive back at the A443 road.

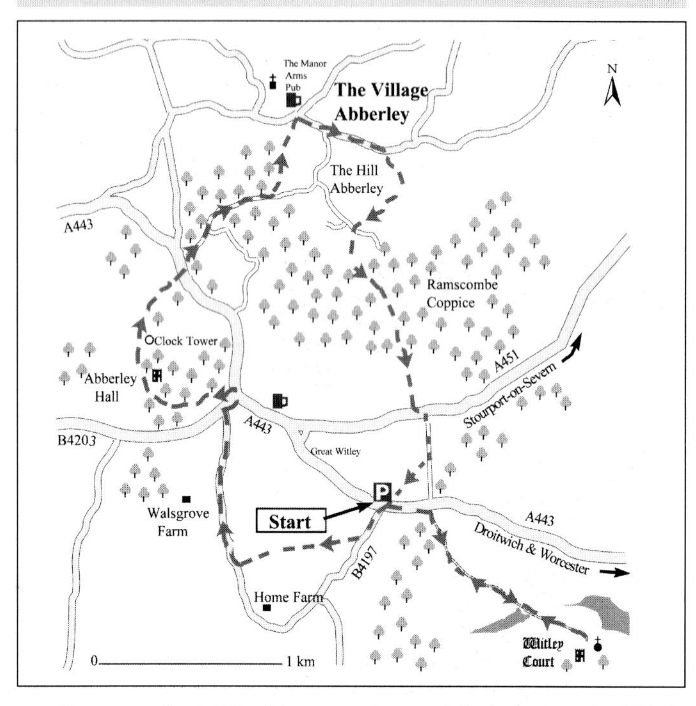

Cross over the A443 with care and ascend the lane opposite. This is fairly steep. In about 600m go left to continue on the Worcestershire Way following the waymarkers over fields and stiles to reach the road in the tiny village of **Abberley**. Go left to the centre of the village and facing you will be the **Manor Arms** pub – over 300 years old and originally owned by the Lord of the Manor.

Until the Middle Ages Abberley was a tiny clearing in the central forest of England. St Michael's Chapel was restored in 1963 and the Saxon tomb cover remains.

From the Manor Arms take the quiet lane opposite for about 500m, then go right to take a farm drive. In 250m bear right and proceed past a farm cottage to go through a black-painted farm gate. Arc right to go over a stile and then follow the right edge of the next field to a lane.

Cross the lane and go over a stile to take a path parallel to the farm drive exiting via a gate. Cross the drive and take a clear path to the left of farm cottages going through a hand-gate and over a stile to enter **Ramscombe Coppice** on Abberley Hill. In about 150m you cross over the Worcestershire Way to continue in a southeast direction and descend steeply on a clear path which emerges from the woodland to pass a disused quarry on the left. You soon arrive at the A451 road by some houses.

Abberley clock tower

Go left along the road pavement for 70m, then cross over the **A451** and descend the lane opposite signed to Martley. After following the road for some 250m, go right through a gateway into a cultivated field and take a clear path that crosses the field diagonally left to emerge via a kissing gate next to the village hall car park in Great Witley.

WALK 36 – Wilmcote and Mary Arden's House

An easy walk in Shakespeare's countryside and by the Stratford-upon-Avon Canal with an opportunity to visit the Bard's home.

Distance:	3 miles (4.8km)
Duration:	Allow 1½ hours
Refreshments:	The Masons Arms and Mary Arden Inn, Wilmcote
Walk Start:	Wilmcote is 3½ miles (5.5km) northwest of Stratford-upon-Avon, left of the A3400 Birmingham road
Car Parking:	Park with consideration by the roadside in the village of Wilmcote (GR 164581)
Terrain:	Easy walking on good flat footpaths
OS Map:	Explorer 205 – Stratford-upon-Avon and Evesham

From the road junction in the middle of the small village of Wilmcote proceed along the Aston Cantlow road, passing behind the outbuildings of **Mary Arden's House** complex. Just before you reach Chapel House, go right over a stile by a gateway and take a clear waymarked path at the rear of the falconry at the Shakespeare Countryside Museum – if you peep through the trees you may see a hawk, an eagle or an owl.

Continue along the path, and to the right you are likely to see donkeys and perhaps long horn cattle – in medieval times the horns of such animals were used to produce windows for the houses. After going over more stiles, you walk to the right of the beautiful mown sports grounds of the village club and then two further stiles take you onto open pastureland to follow the clear path by the left hedge over the next fields. As you approach the end of the second field go right, following waymark posts going generally east and aiming for a metal farm gate near **Broadlow Cottage**.

Proceed through the gate and veer left to go round the derelict building and then take the right-hand field edge path. About 30m

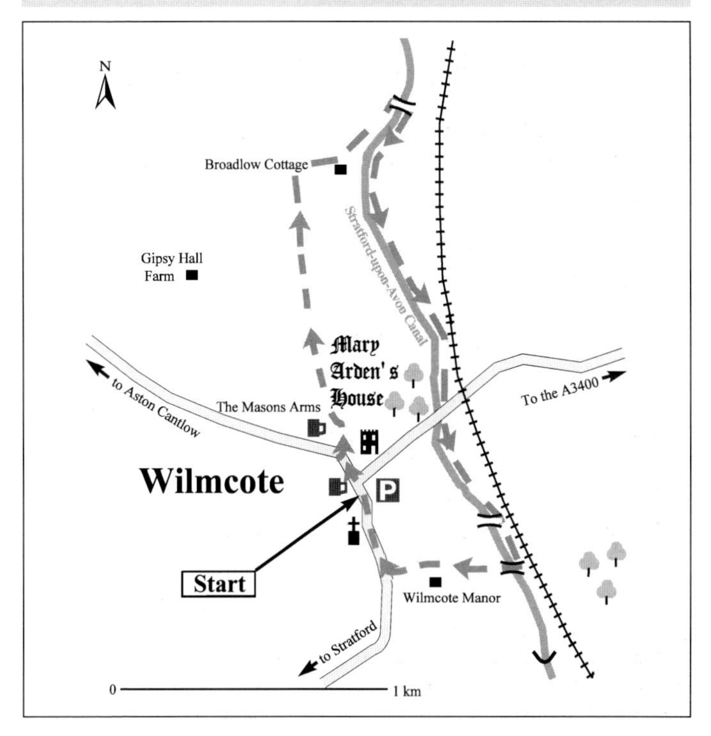

before you reach the field end, go right over a final stile and cross the cast iron bridge over the **Stratford-upon-Avon Canal**. Notice the slit on the farm bridge which was introduced to save the cost of a towpath underneath. In olden days the towing horse would go over the bridge on the towpath and the towing ropes would slip through the towrope slit. As soon as you are over the bridge, go right and follow the canal towpath. This is pleasant, easy walking. Your peace will only be broken by the noise of trains on the nearby railway line and by ornate narrowboats.

As you follow the towpath for the next 1¼ miles (1.8km), you pass a clutter of colourful narrowboats at the Wilmcote Moorings. After passing beneath a road bridge you pass the back of attractive house gardens and then all too soon reach bridge no 60, a second cast iron slit bridge.

Go right over the bridge and take the good track away from the canal. To the left you see **Wilmcote Manor** and then walk at the rear of some large houses before emerging from Manor Drive (a private drive but public footpath) onto the main road in Wilmcote. Here, go right and follow the pavement of the road, passing by the lovely gardens of some very nice houses. Spare time to visit **St Andrew's Church** on the left – a typical English village church.

Continue along the pavement to the road junction and perhaps enjoy refreshments at one of the two inviting village pubs. A visit to Mary Arden's House will complete a pleasant visit.

Owl in the falconry

This was probably the home of Mary Arden, Shakespeare's mother, before she married John Shakespeare when they moved into Stratford-upon-Avon. The Tudor half-timbered farmhouse with its outbuildings are a picture in summer when the roses in the garden form a ground-cover of colour. There is also a falconry (falconry courses are available) and the Shakespeare Countryside Museum to add further interest.

WALK 37 – The Arrow Valley and Ragley Hall

A pleasant walk in attractive Warwickshire countryside to enjoy some lovely views. Nearby Alcester is a Britain in Bloom winner and is always a picture of floral colour and the impressive Ragley Hall is well worth a visit.

Distance:	6 miles (9.6km)
Duration:	Allow about 3 hours
Refreshments:	Pubs and cafes in Alcester
Walk Start:	Arrow is a small village about 1 mile (1.5km) southwest of Alcester. Take the A422 Worcester road from the town. At the junction with the A441 go right onto the B4088 road – the parking layby is on the left in 400m
Car Parking:	Park in the parking layby on the B4088 road (GR 055567)
Terrain:	Easy walking in the Warwickshire countryside
OS Map:	Explorer 205 – Stratford-upon-Avon and Evesham

From the parking layby cross over the B4088 road and take the track opposite towards Nunnery Wood. On reaching the wood, do not enter but go left around its edge for some 1¾ miles (2.8km). This is a pleasant walk by the side of **Weethley Wood**, where bluebells are plentiful and pheasants and deer may keep you company.

At the end of the third field there may be a stream to cross in wet weather – there is a farm bridge which may be used. About 800m beyond this point go left and ascend the right-hand side of the hedge aiming for **Church Farm** and **Weethley Church** on the brow of the hill. Near the buildings go right through a gate and then left through a second gate onto the village road, passing between attractive houses to reach and cross over the A441 road to a stile by a gate into the field opposite. Climb the stile and proceed down the right-hand side of the field, pausing to enjoy a pleasant view towards Alcester.

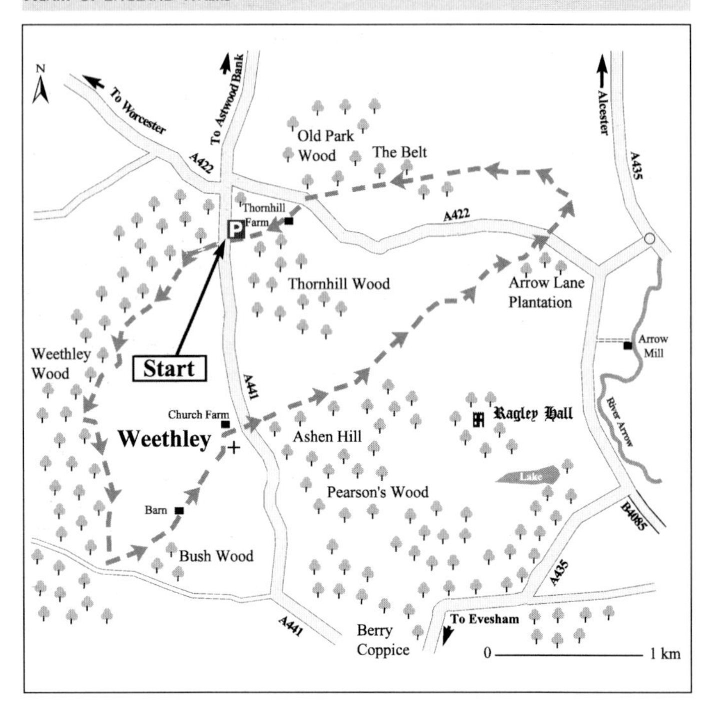

Walk by the left side of the woods on **Ashen Hill** to climb a second stile, then descend gently to pass to the right of a sadly deteriorating half-timbered farm building. Go right at the track, then left by the side of a hedge across the next field to climb a stile on the right (just after Park Cottage). Keep to the left-hand fence – on the right of this next pasture you can get a glimpse of the roofs of Ragley Hall on the rise to the right. Climb the stile at the field end and walk on the other side of the hedge, keeping to the right side of the next field and passing to the right of farm buildings, then follow the path to the **A422** road.

Ragley Hall, built in 1680 and set in some 400 acres of parkland, woodland and gardens, is the home of the Hertford family. The fine building contains much elegant Baroque plasterwork, and Graham Rust's stunning mural 'Temptation' adorns the superb

South Staircase Hall. The delightful gardens were landscaped by Capability Brown.

Cross over the busy A422 road with care and proceed along the waymarked path opposite, keeping by the side of the hedge to a stile in the left field corner. Over the stile (with a pond on the right) bear left along the side of the left hedge of the next field to a gate in its left-hand corner. Go left through the gate keeping to the side of the left hedge/ditch, go through a further gate and over a brick footbridge, then continue by the side of the hedge passing the edge of Newman's Plantation and with Clark's Barn across the fields to the right. At the plantation end proceed through the corner of the trees over a track to continue on a path on the left-hand side of the woodland. You pass an attractive pond to the right in the **Belt** and by the side of **Old Park Wood** to reach a stile and gate onto the A422 road.

Proceed down the drive to **Thornhill Farm** passing to the right of the farm buildings with a large barn and wooden shed on the right. Immediately after the wooden shed go right and proceed through the gate at its rear bearing left by **Thornhill Wood**. Ascend the field to a stile sited in the left-hand fence. Climb the stile and continue up the other side of the fence to two gates which lead onto the B4088 road where your car is parked.

WALK 38 – Shakespeare's Stratford

A pleasant walk around beautiful Stratford-upon-Avon and an opportunity to join the many people from all over the world who make a pilgrimage to the Bard's home town. The route takes you past the main Shakespeare attractions and encompasses a delightful short walk into the nearby countryside for a fine view over the town – an opportunity to see the best of Stratford-upon-Avon.

Distance:	4 miles (6.4km)
Duration:	Allow 2 to 2½ hours' walking (overall 4 to 5 hours)
Refreshments:	Variety of establishments in Stratford-upon-Avon itself; the Bell Inn, Shottery
Car Parking:	Several pay and display parks in Stratford-upon-Avon: Windsor Street, Market Place, multi-storey at Bridgefoot
Terrain:	Easy walking on good flat footpaths
OS Map:	Explorer 205 – Stratford-upon-Avon and Evesham

Start the walk in pedestrianised Henley Street by the Shakespeare Birth Place Trust and the entrance to **Shakespeare's Birthplace**.

No visit to Stratford is complete without a visit to Shakespeare's Birthplace. This is where the great man was born and where his father lived as a glovemaker from the 1550s. William, born in 1564, was brought up here. Today the building retains much of its original structure and has a lovely garden at its rear.

From the Birthplace walk along Henley Street past the 15th Century Public Library building and continue until you reach the road island at the junction of Henley Street/Bridge Street and High Street. Bear right and proceed along the pavement of High Street where you will see many fine timber-framed buildings. **Harvard House** and the Garrick Inn are on your right.

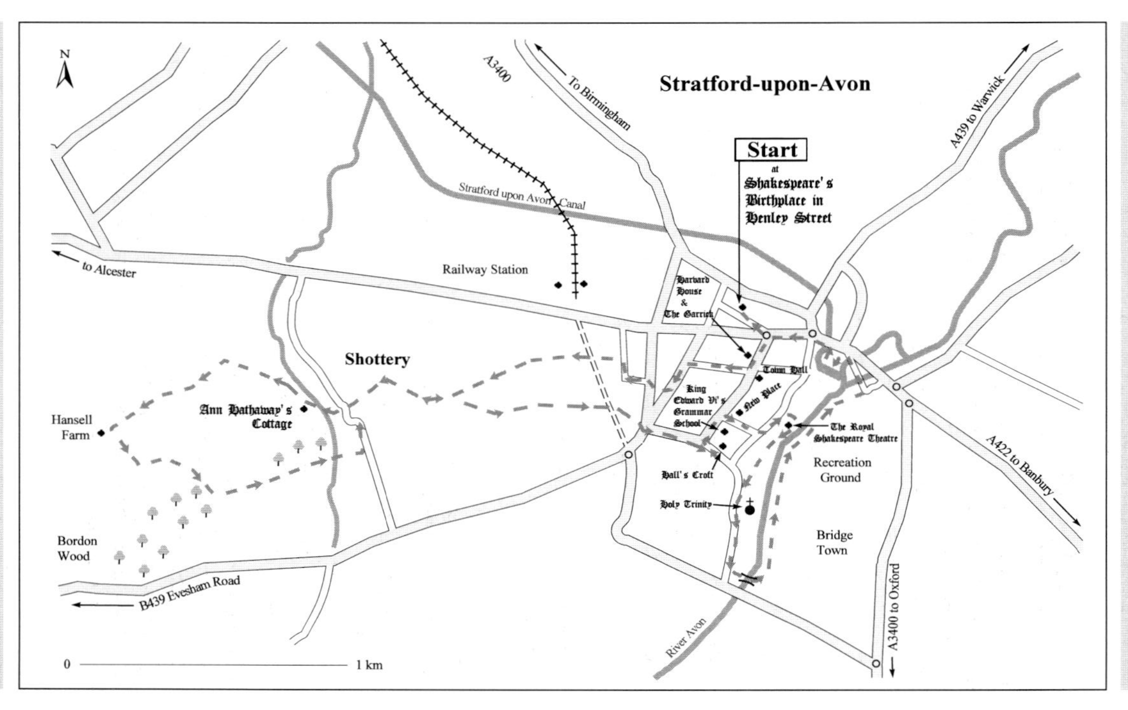

Stratford-upon-Avon
Start
at
Shakespeare's Birthplace in Henley Street
A439 to Warwick
A422 to Banbury
A3400 to Oxford
To Birmingham
A3400
Stratford upon Avon Canal
Railway Station
to Alcester
Harvard House & The Garrick
Town Hall
King Edward VI's Grammar School
New Place
The Royal Shakespeare Theatre
Hall's Croft
Holy Trinity
Recreation Ground
Bridge Town
River Avon
Shottery
Ann Hathaway's Cottage
Hansell Farm
Bordon Wood
B439 Evesham Road
N
0
1 km

You can visit Harvard House free of charge – see the Neish Pewter collection and inspect the old 16th-century Elizabethan timber-fronted building which has the initials of its first owners inscribed over the richly carved front door. It was rebuilt in 1596 when it was the home of Katherine Rogers, mother of John Harvard, founder of Harvard University in the USA. Adjoining Harvard House is the richly carved timber-fronted Garrick Inn where you may wish to imbibe.

From Harvard House proceed along High Street then go right at the impressive town hall building. The Cotswold Stone town hall dates from 1767. On its front are the words 'God save the King' and this relates to George III who was king at the time the building was erected. On the Sheep Street frontage is a statue of William Shakespeare, a gift from the actor David Garrick in 1769.

As you go right you enter Ely Street which leads you to Rother Street. Here go left and cross over the street to enter the small triangle-shaped gardens. Walk through these pleasant gardens to arrive in Grove Road. Cross over Grove Road and proceed up Albany Road opposite. As you round the road corner look out for a footpath sign to Ann Hathaway's Cottage. At the sign go left and take the clear footpath which leads between Shottery Fields. Continue along the tarmac footpath past the children's play area and bearing right at its end. Follow the signs towards Ann Hathaway's Cottage via Tavern Lane. This takes you by some very attractive period houses and by the side of a horticultural centre to arrive by a road island near to the Bell Inn in **Shottery**.

Cross over the road and enter a small garden area to the right of Cottage Lane. This will take you off the road and leads down to a footbridge over Shottery Brook and a delightful view of **Ann Hathaway's Cottage**. A visit is well worthwhile.

This picturesque timber-framed and thatched cottage was the home of Shakespeare's wife before their marriage. Ann Hathaway, daughter of Richard, was born in 1556 and married William Shakespeare in 1582. At that time Shottery was little more than a cluster of homesteads sited on the edge of the Arden Forest. Today, the cottage is one of the most famous buildings in England and has become a shrine of international literary pilgrimage This much

The old and the new Pershore bridges (Walk 42)

View from the Worcester Beacon (Walk 43)

View from the topograph on Dover's Hill (Walk 44)

Lower Lode Hotel by the River Severn (Walk 48)

visited olde worlde property with its lovely whitewashed walls is set in delightful gardens.

Leave the cottage via a garden trail to the Shottery Brook Walk and this brings you back onto Cottage Lane about 100m above the cottage entrance. If you do not wish to visit Ann Hathaway's Cottage continue past the building up Cottage Lane. In about 150m go left up a farm drive signed **Hansell Farm** – Footpath. Proceed up the drive with fields of blue linseed oil plants either side. Just before you reach the farm complex, go left through a field corner kissing gate and take the clear

The Gower Memorial, Stratford

path along the top of the field to reach and go through a hand-gate near an attractive bungalow. Just through the gate is a stone memorial to Charles Turriff who lived on the farm for 40 years.

Now veer left to take a path between blue linseed oil plants where you can enjoy an interesting view over Stratford-upon-Avon with the Holy Trinity Church and the obelisk on Welcome Hill clearly visible on the horizon. The path arcs right to enter trees then in about 50m go sharp left on a path heading northeast by the side of deciduous trees. Soon you are walking by a conifer plantation before arriving on the edge of Shottery. After going over a small bridge you arrive at the road by St Andrew's National School, 1870. Go left and at the road junction you see the inviting building of the Bell Inn where you may choose to stop for refreshments.

Go right and proceed towards Stratford-upon-Avon, pausing at the sharp bend in the road to see the beautiful thatched cottages on the left. Now continue around the corner and go left along the footpath which leads you back to Shottery Fields. At the field entrance bear right, following the footpath sign to Halls Croft. This path leads you along the back of residential houses until you arrive back in Stratford-upon-Avon at Evesham Place.

Cross over the pedestrian crossing and take Chestnut Walk proceeding into Old Town where you find the impressive **Hall's Croft**.

A Shakespearean period house that was named after William's son-in-law, Dr John Hall, who married Susanna Shakespeare in 1607. Delightful gardens surround this timber-framed, lath and plaster structure that has a tiled roof with many gables surmounted by superb chimney stacks. Inside are displays of period furniture and paintings plus a fascinating exhibition of medical practice in Dr Hall's day.

From Hall's Croft return to the top of Old Town and go right along Church Street. You pass the Shakespeare Institute on the left then almshouses, **King Edward VI School** and the Guild Chapel on the right.

Built in 1417–18, this was the grammar school where William Shakespeare and the author of this book were both educated – Shakespeare's plays reveal a clear knowledge of the school curriculum. The Guild Chapel is where the members of the medieval Guild of the Holy Cross met. Although the wall paintings were whitewashed over during the Reformation they have been partly restored. The nave and altar date from about 1269. The superb row of almshouses set by the grammar school were built in 1427 to provide a home for the aged and infirm people of the Guild.

At the junction of Church/Chapel Streets and Scholars/Chapel Lane, **New Place** and Nash's House are set on the right corner opposite the Guild Chapel.

New Place was purchased by Shakespeare in 1597. He retired to live in the house and died here in 1616. The original house was demolished in 1759 and only the foundations remain, now set in the lovely Elizabethan-style knott garden – a delight of floral colour in the summer. Nash's House is set immediately next to New Place. Thomas Nash, who owned Nash's House, married Shakespeare's granddaughter, Elizabeth, who was the last direct descendant of the great man. Do spare time to meander the beautiful gardens.

Before you proceed through New Place gardens spare a few moments to see the frontage of the Shakespeare Hotel and then continue down Chapel Lane to find the famous **Royal Shakespeare Theatre**. Bear left, cross over Waterside and you will see the theatre. You can enter the foyer. Continue to the River Avon and go right to find the balcony of the theatre, where refreshments can be taken. If you continue you pass by the Swan Theatre and can walk through the attractive Theatre Gardens. Continue past the Dirty Duck pub and the small ferry point. You pass by The Other Place and there are wonderful brass rubbing opportunities. At the end of the gardens you arrive in Old Town where go left to enter the churchyard of **Holy Trinity Church**.

This impressive church was originally built in the 13th century and has later additions (the nave was rebuilt in the 15th century). The chancel contains Shakespeare's grave and the church has become another pilgrimage site. Set on the banks of the beautiful River Avon, its superb 18th-century spire is a Stratford landmark.

Proceed out of the rear of the churchyard and continue south down a lane which eventually reaches the Old Mill (converted to residential apartments). After passing the Old Mill, go across the footbridge over the River Avon then bear left to take the far bank of the attractive river. You pass by a fine weir and continue along the riverbank until you reach the old tramway bridge from where there is a fine view over the river towards the Royal Shakespeare Theatre building – the bridge itself is most scenic. Walk over the bridge, pausing at intervals to enjoy the riverside scene. All too soon you are walking to the right of the Basin, which is usually a colourful sight with attractive narrow-boats on what is the start of the Stratford-upon-Avon Canal. There is a famous statue of the Bard, the Gower Memorial.

Continue on to Bridgefoot and then walk up Bridge Street. At the top bear right into Henley Street and the Birthplace, where your walk began.

WALK 39 – Fenny Compton and Farnborough Hall

This attractive walk will take you along the towpath of the Coventry Canal and then over attractive countryside that passes near to the impressive Farnborough Hall (National Trust). There are fine views of Farnborough village and the surrounding countryside as you return to Fenny Compton. The route continues over cultivated fields to reach Northend before passing through the delightful Burton Dasset Country Park on the final stretch of walking.

Distance:	10 miles (16km)
Duration:	Allow 5 to 6 hours
Refreshments:	The Merrie Lion Inn, Fenny Compton, and the Butcher's Arms, Farnborough
Walk Start:	Fenny Compton is 16 miles (26km) north of Banbury off the A423 Coventry road. Near the Wharf, go left into the village
Car Parking:	Park by the roadside (with consideration) near the Merrie Lion Inn, Fenny Compton
Terrain:	Easy walking but with a few undulations
OS Map:	Explorer 191 – Banbury, Bicester and Chipping Norton

From the Merrie Lion Inn, proceed up the Wormleighton Road. Where the road bends right, go left over a stile and take a path at the back of houses in a general northeast direction. Continue over stiles across a lane leading to a Severn Trent works location and over two further stiles to go beneath a dismantled line. Proceed ahead to reach a further stile that leads beneath the **mainline railway** bridge. Continue on the clear path over a cultivated field which soon arcs right to go through a gate and to cross the Wormleighton Road once again. Now you descend to the towpath of the **Oxford Canal** – by a mooring area which is usually lined with attractive narrowboats.

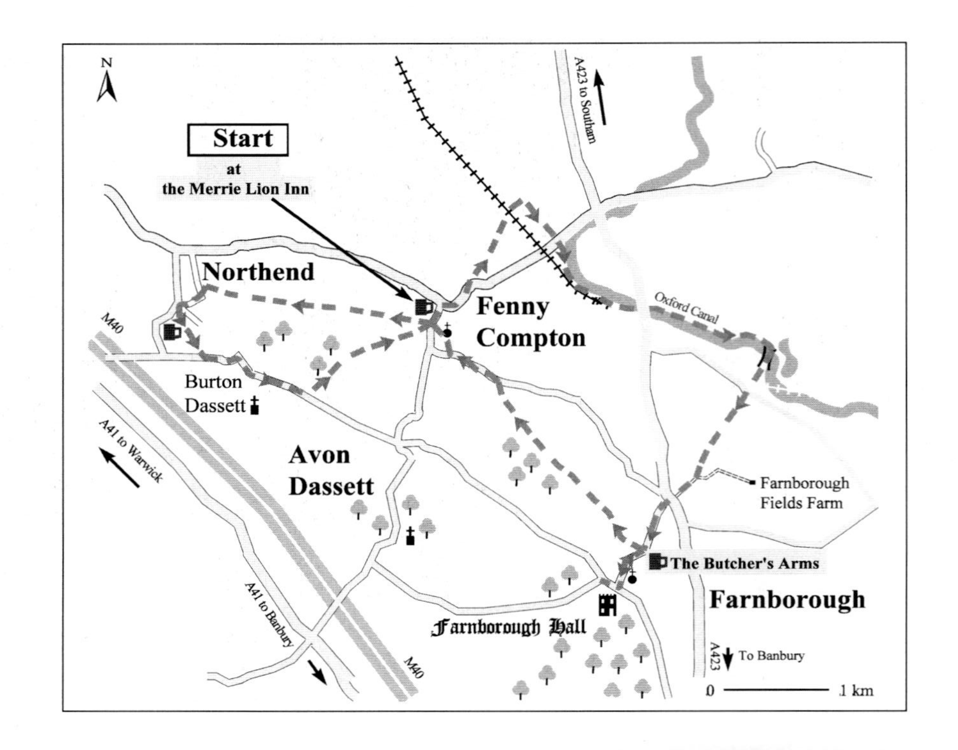
N
Start
at
the Merrie Lion Inn
A423 to Southam
Northend
Fenny
Compton
Oxford Canal
M40
Burton
Dassett
A41 to Warwick
Avon
Dassett
Farnborough
Fields Farm
The Butcher's Arms
Farnborough
A41 to Banbury
Farnborough Hall
M40
A423
To Banbury
0
1 km

Initially you walk to the right of the canal and cross over canal bridge no 137, then take the left bank towpath proceeding beneath the A423 road bridge. The canal narrows where there was once a tunnel and then widens once again and gradually pulls away from the mainline railway. At canal bridge no 139 go right through a gate and walk over the bridge to proceed in a general southwest direction on a clear track/path. You go through a pair of gates by the mainline railway – take great care when crossing – then continue over pastureland maintaining the southwest direction over a series of fields and going through several farm gates. In about 500m you see **Farnborough Fields Farm** to your far left and then soon reach a farm drive. Here, go right to reach the A423 road.

Farnborough Hall (National Trust)

Cross over the A423 and ascend the road opposite which leads into the village of ***Farnborough****. You walk down through the village, passing the* ***Butcher's Arms*** *pub (set back behind a wall to the left), to visit* ***Farnborough Hall*** *at the end of the village – bear right at the road junction and you soon reach the entrance to the hall on your left.*

This lovely home of the Holbech family was built in the mid 18th century in honey-coloured stone with superb interior plasterwork. There is a fine garden containing 18th-century temples, a terrace walk and an obelisk – a delightful house to visit.

Return to the road near the Butcher's Arms opposite to which go left on a signed footpath between houses to go over a stile into pastureland. Now you walk in a general northwest direction over attractive undulating fields. You ascend Windmill Hill and are rewarded with a fine retrospective view over the village of Farnborough. At the top maintain the same line to go over a footbridge and then ascend Hall's Hill ahead with pleasing views all around and walking a clear path over cultivated fields. Proceed through a metal kissing gate and over a small footbridge to reach a lane. Now go left and follow the lane towards **Fenny Compton**.

As you approach the village, the church is visible to the right and you go right over a stile to take a field up towards it. Aim for a gate to the left of the **church** which leads into Dog Lane. Go right and walk through the village, enjoying the pleasing appearance of the Horton Stone houses/cottages.

Now go left and take a clearly waymarked path going generally west towards Northend. Take the path over a mixture of pastureland and cultivated fields and over several stiles. As you approach **Northend** you go through a couple of kissing gates before arriving at a road in the village. Here go left and in about 100m go left again over stiles to enter the area of the delightful **Burton Dassett** Country Park. You quickly reach the park road that leads up to the 'Beacon' where there is an impressive view which stretches as far as the Malvern Hills, but is sadly spoilt by the noise of the M40 road below.

Go left to walk along the park road and ascend past the White House. After about 300m of superb scenic walking, go left through a hand-gate to descend by a hedge with a fine view ahead – this embraces Gredenton Hill and Fenny Compton. The path arcs gently right to go through a gate then arcs left to a further gate before continuing in its general northeast direction. All too soon you arrive back in the village of Fenny Compton, where go left to return to the Merrie Lion and the centre of the village.

WALK 40 – Upton House and the Edgehill Walk

A pleasant meander along the ridge of Edgehill to enjoy some fine views of the valley below and an opportunity to visit the impressive 17th-century Upton House – a delightful mansion house that was donated to the National Trust by the 2nd Viscount Bearsted.

Distance:	5¾ miles (9.2km)
Duration:	Allow 2½ hours' walking
Refreshments:	The Castle Inn, Edgehill
Walk Start:	Sun Rising Hill is about 10 miles (16km) northwest of Banbury on the A423 Stratford road. To get to the main start in Ratley continue to the next turn left off the A423 – in about a mile (2km) go right into the village and find the car park on the left by cottages. Sugarswell Lane is to the left at the top of the hill.
Car Parking:	Park in the parking area in front of cottages in the village of Ratley. (GR 380476) If a large group is travelling by car you can park on the grass verge in Sugarswell Lane, Edgehill (GR 358452) and can start your walk at paragraph 3.
Terrain:	Generally easy walking but the footpaths can be muddy underfoot in wet weather
OS Map:	Explorer 191 – Banbury, Bicester and Chipping Norton

From the parking area in Ratley, walk the road going north west towards Edgehill. At the road junction cross the road and follow the waymarkers of a path the descends via steps into the woodland. You are now on the Centenary and MacMillan Ways and should follow their waymarkers through the trees on a well trodden footpath along the edge of the famous hill - you will have glimpses of the valley below

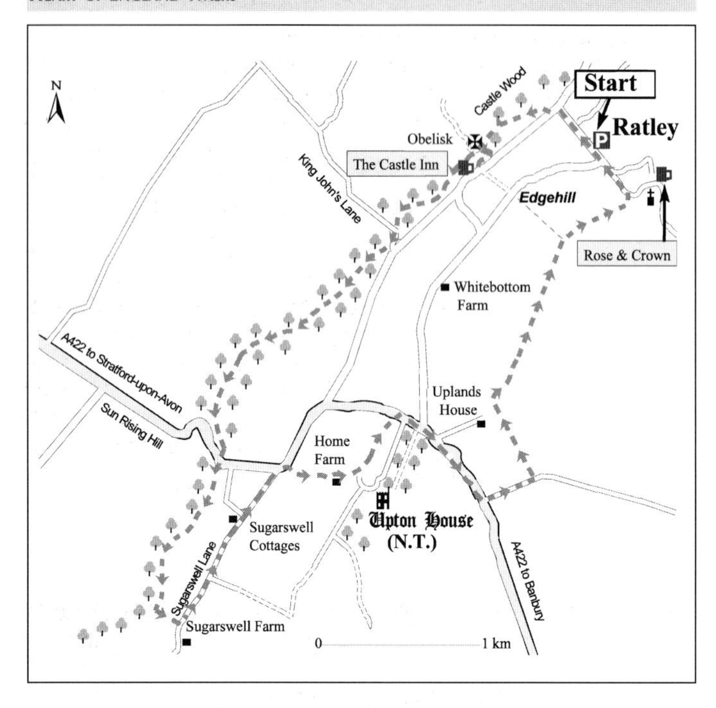

through the trees. After about 400m of woodland walking bear right to visit the **Obelisk** to Charles Chambers. The Obelisk was erected in 1854 to commemorate the Battle of Waterloo.

Return to the waymarked path and continue along the escarpment of Edgehill and soon you will see a huge old castle buildings up to your left. The Castle Inn has been converted into an Inn, and its two fortified turrets are joined by a bridge which was built in 1992 – the main turret is very high and most impressive. You may wish to pause in your walk to enjoy the Castle Inn and have refreshment. Return to the main path and continue along the escarpment with the hedge on your left and trees on your right, pausing periodically to enjoy a superb view of the valley through the trees. After walking the escarpment for about 1¼ miles/2km you reach the A422 road at the very top of **Sun Rising Hill**.

Cross over the road and continue on the waymarked track, initially bearing right between the buildings of stables and then left to continue along a track to go through a gate to open land and the most superb view of Tysoe and the surrounding countryside. Pause to admire this view at your leisure, then continue through a second gate to take a path on the edge of the woods. In about 150m go left through a gate to walk by the side of a hedge and to arrive back in Sugarswell Lane.

Proceed left along Sugarswell Lane towards the junction with the A422 (Stratford to Banbury Road) at the top of Sun Rising Hill. Here, go right and in 10 yards go right again through a gate and walk a path by the side of a stone wall then bear left towards Home Farm. Proceed on the clear path to the left of the farm buildings and diagonally to go through two gates. Then bear left by the side of a fence to a stile in the far right corner of the field to arrive back at the A422 road. Go right along the wide grass verge of the busy road pausing at the gates of Upton House to view the front of this National Trust House.

Upton House

Upton House (NT). Spare time to visit the impressive late 17th-century mansion which contains one of the finest collections of pictures and objets d'art in the UK and has a delightful garden.

Continue along the grass verge for about 600 yards then cross over the busy A422 with care and proceed down a lane on the left. Walk down this quiet lane for about 300 yards, then go left along a signed path keeping to the left of the hedge. Proceed over two fields towards Uplands House and Uplands Farm and go to the right of the buildings to soon arrive in open fields. Descend the path to a gate and into a valley and then make a fairly testing ascent by the side of the hedge passing an old dilapidated barn on your right. Proceed by the field hedge and at a junction of paths proceed ahead over a stile to the right of an old barn and descend pastureland now going north east to a further stile in the far right corner of the field. Ahead of you is Ratley village and there is a fine view of rolling Warwickshire countryside to enjoy as you descend to go over the stile before arriving at a final stile set to the left of Manor Farm building. This will lead you back into the village of Ratley. To your right is a lovely thatched cottage and beautiful old village church to admire or you may wish to go left up the road to return to your car.

WALK 41 – Mickleton and the Hidcote Manor Hill Walk

This walk through undulating countryside provides gentle views and pleasing Cotswold landscape together with an opportunity to visit the famous Hidcote Manor Gardens (National Trust).

Distance:	5 miles (8km)
Duration:	Allow 3 hours
Refreshments:	The Kings Arms Inn, an old coaching inn, is a regular eating house for local walkers. It is on the B4632 road in the village of Mickleton
Walk Start:	Mickleton is about 9 miles (14.5km) south of Stratford-upon-Avon on the A4632 road
Car Parking:	Park your car near St Lawrence's Church in Mickleton (GR 162435)
Terrain:	There is one hill climb otherwise the walking is easy. Parts may be muddy in wet weather
OS Map:	Explorer 205 – Stratford-upon-Avon and Evesham

Leave your car in Mickleton in the small parking area near St Lawrence's Church and commence the walk by crossing the lane, going left then right up a grass slope immediately after the drive to Field House. Now follow the signed path, proceeding through a kissing gate and crossing a field to a gate in its far right corner. Continue along the path through the trees to a further gate at their end, then ascend gently up the left side of a field to go over/through a stile/gate. Once through the stile/gate, bear right to join the Heart of England Way and to commence a short but steep ascent to a gate onto a lane near Baker's Hill. Pause here for a fine retrospective view of Mickleton then cross the lane and ascend the stepped path through trees to a stile. Go right along **Baker's Hill** with trees to the right before entering the wood. Follow the track inside the edge of the wood, walking to its end and then crossing a field and bearing left around a barn/farm buildings to reach a narrow lane. Go right along the lane for about 400m passing

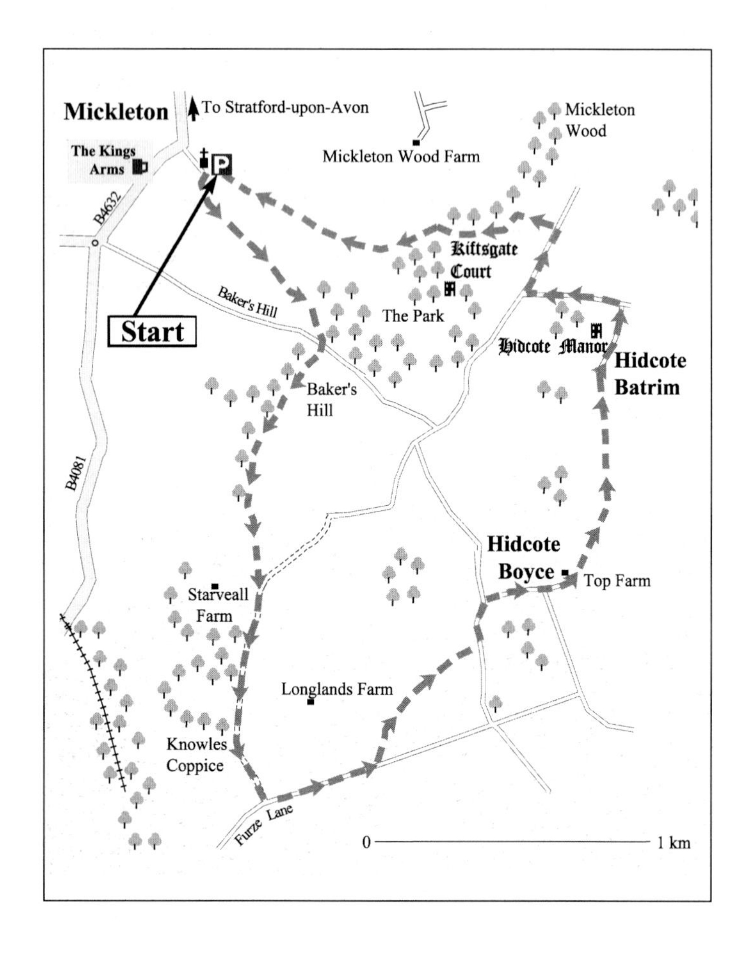
Mickleton
To Stratford-upon-Avon
Mickleton Wood
Mickleton Wood Farm
The Kings Arms
B4632
Kiftsgate Court
Baker's Hill
Start
The Park
Hidcote Manor
Hidcote Batrim
Baker's Hill
B4081
Hidcote Boyce
Top Farm
Starveall Farm
Longlands Farm
Knowles Coppice
Furze Lane
0
1 km

Starveall Farm, and with **Knowles Coppice** on the right, to reach Furze Lane.

Go left (leaving the Heart of England Way) along **Furze Lane** for about 220m then go left again through a gate onto a path that arcs northeast to a stile then crosses a second field to a further stile onto the Hidcote Road. Here pause to look back over the Cotswold hills and to see Broadway Tower at the crest, then go left along the road for about 100m. Go right at the crossroads and meander through the sleepy and pretty hamlet of **Hidcote Boyce** – a real pleasure when the flowers of spring are at their peak. Proceed to **Top Farm**, go through a kissing gate and then walk diagonally left over the field on a clear path to a further stile. Continue on the path in a north direction along the edge of a very large field with a fruit farm to your left as you reach a gateway onto a lane in **Hidcote Batrim**.

Thatched cottage in Hidcote Batrim

Walk down the road of this picturesque village of thatched sandstone buildings, passing a 1918 war memorial, the village duck pond and the entrance to **Hidcote Manor** (NT).

During a visit to one of England's great gardens you can expect to meet many people. The gardens are a masterpiece of design being created by Major Lawrence Johnston. It is like a series of gardens within a garden, each with a different character and separated by walls and hedges. Superb rare shrubs and trees and outstanding herbacious borders – careful planting ensures that you can enjoy a fine display of colour throughout the year.

Go left at the junction of lanes and walk down the entrance drive going west for some 200m to the Hidcote Road. Here, go right along the road for 250m then go left to descend a track into **Mickleton Wood** – this is steep in parts. Continue to a field gate which go through into pastureland where you can enjoy a fine view over Mickleton and the surrounding countryside. Follow the waymark arrow that leads left towards Mickleton. You go over a stile and walk by the side of a hedge until you reach a hand-gate. Cross the field heading towards St Lawrence's Church and you soon arrive back at the car park near the church.

WALK 42 – Pershore Abbey Walk

A pleasant walk to experience the fruit-growing area of the Vale of Evesham with fine views which embrace Clee Hill and the Malvern and Bredon hills. Tyddesley Woods date back some 6000 years although in the 13th century the Abbott of Westminster made it into a deer park – today it is fine woodland and pleasant to meander. The return to Pershore is on a delightful footpath along the bank of the River Avon where fishermen, canoes and motorboats contribute to the rural scene. Throughout the walk the vision of Pershore Abbey is never far away and there is the opportunity to visit the town and its superb abbey as you return to Pershore.

Distance:	5 miles (8km)
Duration:	Allow 2½ hours
Refreshments:	Pubs and cafes in Pershore. The New Inn in High Street is particularly attractive
Walk Start:	Pershore is 3½ miles (5.5km) west of Evesham
Car Parking:	Abbey Park pay and display car park in Abbey Road, Pershore (GR 947458)
Terrain:	Easy walking on generally good way-marked footpaths. The paths in Tyddesley Woods may be muddy in wet weather
OS Map:	Explorer 190 – Malvern Hills and Bredon Hill

From the car park, turn your back on Pershore Abbey and aim for a tarmac path to the right of the road entrance to **Abbey Park Middle School**. Take the path at the back of houses, bearing right and then left to reach New Road. Go right, cross over the main road and continue up a residential road opposite – it is named **Holloway**. About 600m from the main road, go left at a footpath sign (opposite to house number 86) and proceed past a corrugated asbestos farm building onto a wide green track. To the right the Malvern Hills are on the horizon, while Bredon Hill is prominent to the left as you follow the good track for about 400m. Go right at the junction of paths and head towards Tyddesley Woods.

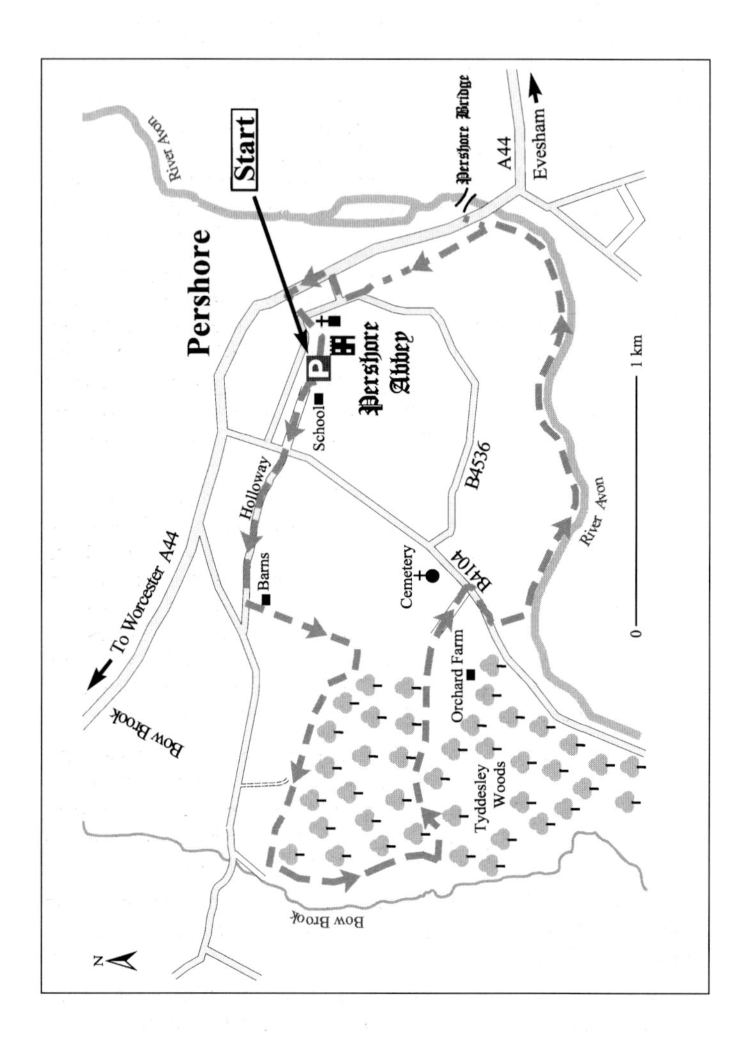

Start
Pershore
River Avon
Pershore Bridge
A44
Evesham
P
Pershore Abbey
School
Holloway
B4536
Barns
Cemetery
B4104
River Avon
To Worcester A44
Orchard Farm
Tyddesley Woods
Bow Brook
Bow Brook
0
1 km
N

Bear right at the trees and follow the outside perimeter of the woodland going over a couple of field stiles. There is a pleasant countryside view to the right and you reach a further stile with a picnic area to the right. Go over the stile and now take a clear path just inside the woodland. At the bottom of the wood go over a further stile and take the clear green path at the top of fruit trees and with **Bow Brook** some 100m to the right. The field on the far side of the brook is a delight of linseed oil blue in June/July. Take the pleasant green path for about 700m where you will reach a stile into **Tyddesley Woods**.

Go over the stile and go left on a clear path up through the trees proceeding in a generally east direction through the fine woodland. Exit the wood via a hand-gate and walk by the right hedge to the field end. Now go over a stile to the right by a track to **Orchard Farm** on the right. Continue on the other side of the hedge on a clear path which leads to a stile/gate to the left of a beautiful thatched cottage. Proceed over the stile and follow a lane descending gently to the B4104 opposite Three Springs Nursery.

Cross over the B4104 with care and go right taking the grass verge for about 150m. Now go left over a stile and follow the footpath to reach the banks of the **River Avon**. Go left and follow the riverbank footpath for some 1¼ miles/2km until you arrive at **Pershore Bridge**. Fishermen are likely to be along the banks of the river as they seek to fill their nets with bream, perch or roach, while tourists in canoes and motorboats force swans, ducks and moorhens to dive for cover. Walk on to the new bridge (on the A44) and take time to admire the picturesque 14th-century bridge which was built by the monks of Pershore.

Now return to the riverside footpath and go right along a green path which runs almost parallel with the A44 road. At the field end go over a stile and follow a hedged path by allotments. Continue on this path line to pass by a cricket pitch, then go right and then left to pass through a new housing estate to reach Defford Road in Pershore.

Go right along Defford Road until you reach Broad Street at the end of which is a group of Georgian houses built in about 1810. Go right along the very wide Broad Street.

Until 1836 there were houses and a shambles in the centre of Broad Street. On the far right corner note the fine Royal Arcade shopping centre. The stone-faced building (about 1830) has superb ornate ironwork on its balcony and there is a blue Civic Society plaque on the wall commemorating the fact that 'this Regency building was formerly The Royal Three Nuns Hotel visited in 1830 by Princess Victoria and her mother, the Duchess of Kent'. At the top of Broad Street you find Regency balconies on Brown's and Ogle's.

Go left along the High Street past some more fine old buildings.

You pass by the Angel Inn and Posting House, a superb old coaching inn with an elegant façade. The three shops with bow windows were the windows of the Ship Inn recently converted into shops.

Go left down Church Street at the end of which the magnificent **Pershore Abbey** is set in Abbey Park – a truly delightful scene. Close to the abbey is St Andrew's, once a medieval church which served the tenants of the Abbot of Westminster but now converted into a parish centre. Spare time to visit the very fine abbey.

Pershore Abbey

Founded in AD 689, the abbey became a Benedictine Monastery in the 10th century. However, it soon suffered heavy financial losses and together with many local estates was made over to the Abbey of Westminster. In 1223 the Norman presbytery was damaged by fire and at the end of the 14th century the Norman tower was replaced by the current tower which it is believed was designed by the architect of Salisbury Cathedral. The Gothic tower and choir remain intact.

The Abbey Park pay and display car park is at the back of Abbey Park.

Walk 43 – A Malvern Hills Experience

An opportunity to walk the Malvern Hills, one of the major landmarks of the Heart of England. The easier short walk offers a taste of the Malverns with a final ascent of the Herefordshire Beacon on the way back to the car park. The long walk is a truly magnificent walk of the main range of the Malvern Hills with some of the most superb views in the area.

Distance:	Short walk 4¾ miles (7.6km), long walk 9 miles (14.4km)
Duration:	Short walk 2¾ hours, long walk 5 hours
Refreshments:	The Malvern Hills Hotel, British Camp, is by the car park. Short walk – the Singing Kettle Cafe; long walk – the Wyche Inn, Upper Wyche; the Brewsters Arms, West Malvern
Walk Start:	From Malvern take the A449 road towards Ledbury. At the peak of the Malvern Hills you reach a large car park at British Camp
Car Parking:	Pay and display car park (toilets) at British Camp (GR 763404)
Terrain:	Short walk – fairly easy but with one climb over the Herefordshire Beacon. Long walk – hilly
OS Map:	Explorer 190 – Malvern Hills and Bredon Hill

The Malvern Hills were formed more than 600 million years ago by heat and changes below the earth's surface during volcanic activity. Approximately 8 miles (12km) long and up to ½ mile (1km) wide the hills rise to a height of 1395ft/425m and today provide a major landmark for the Heart of England. On top of the hills, a medieval Shire Ditch was built between 1287 and 1291 by the red-headed Gilbert de Clare (Earl of Gloucester). The Red Earl's Dyke was constructed to divide his hunting forests from those of the Bishop of Hereford. It was built in such a position as to allow the Bishop's deer to get over onto the Earl's land but they were

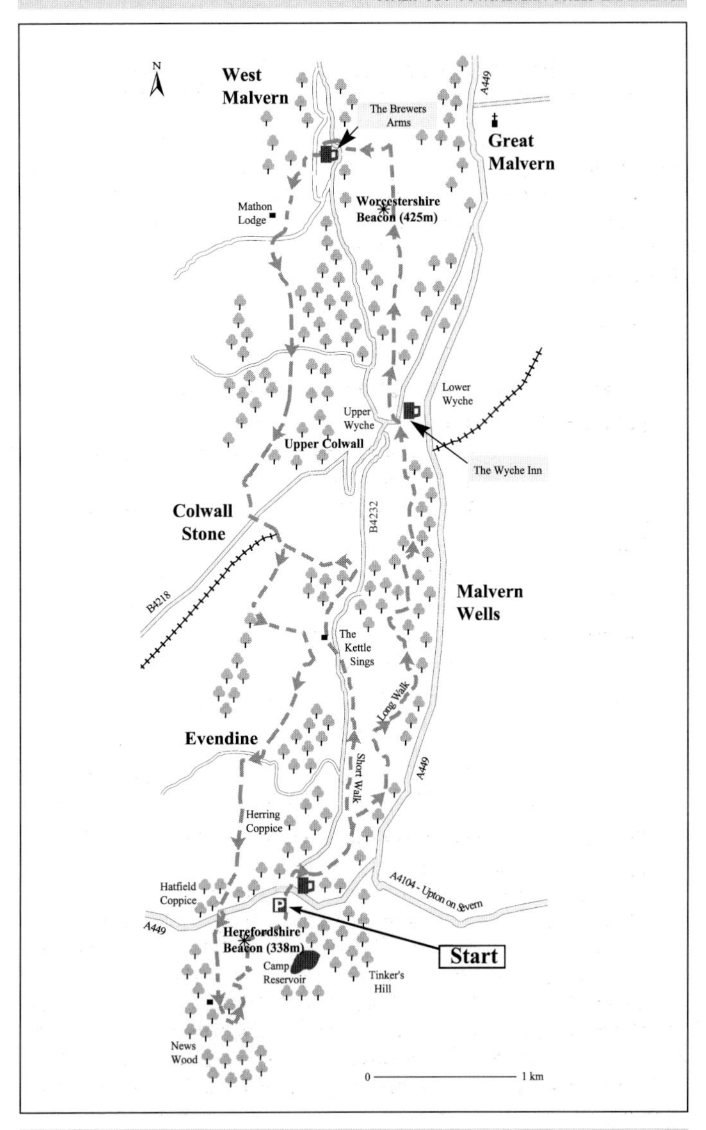
West Malvern
The Brewers Arms
A449
Great Malvern
Mathon Lodge
Worcestershire Beacon (425m)
Lower Wyche
Upper Wyche
Upper Colwall
The Wyche Inn
Colwall Stone
B4232
B4218
Malvern Wells
The Kettle Sings
Long Walk
Evendine
Short Walk
A449
Herring Coppice
A4104 - Upton on Severn
Hatfield Coppice
A449
Herefordshire Beacon (338m)
Start
Camp Reservoir
Tinker's Hill
News Wood
0
1 km

unable to return to the Bishop's forests. Today Shire Ditch is still clearly visible and runs virtually the whole length of the Malverns.

From the car park at British Camp, cross over the **A449** road with care. Toilets are on the left as you take the B4232 road past the Malvern Hills Hotel. Just past the hotel building bear right off the B4232 onto a clear stone path. The path leads through Wynds Point car park and ascends to Shire Ditch where bear left to walk its ridge. At the first junction of some six paths by a bench facing east over Upper Well, the short and long walks go their separate ways.

Short Walk

Continue up the main path to the left of Shire Ditch going generally north. There are fine views to the west as the path arcs to the left. Take the first left fork and descend gently to cross over the **B4232** road. Now take the lane opposite which runs generally parallel with the main road and passes by the **Singing Kettle** – a pleasant place to have a cup of tea with a view. From here continue along the quiet lane for about 300m and at a bend in the lane go left over a stile to descend through trees on a path that arcs left for some 400m to reach a path junction. Here there is a pleasing view of the valley below. Go right for 60m then left over a stile to descend two fields, walking by the right field hedge and going over a further stile. At the bottom of the second field go left and join the path of the Worcestershire Way (route description continues at **Completion of Walks**).

Long Walk

Go right just past the bench seat and descend a delightful path. At the first path junction, bear left and then keep to the main path generally above trees. The path soon circles a large old quarry area where wild flowers abound on the hills. Continue past a narrow path to the right (this leads sharply downhill to Upper Welland) and follow what becomes a balcony path with a superb view to the right (east) over Upper Welland with its old abbey and with **Malvern Wells** to its left. The path enters woodland and then soon you go right onto a lower path that appears to run parallel with the higher path but gently descends to a road by the Holy Well – perhaps take the opportunity to drink a cup of pure Malvern Water. If you miss the path do not worry because all of the higher paths lead to the B4218 road. Continue past

Holy Well

the Holy Well building where you join a path which continues north through pleasant woodland. Keep to the main path which soon emerges from the trees to offer a view over **Upper Wyche** with a panorama beyond. The path ascends and soon you emerge between buildings to arrive at a corner of the B4218 road – the **Wyche Inn** is on the other side of the road if you are ready for refreshments. Cross over the road and ascend the railed tarmac path opposite signed 'Leading to 74-90 Wyche Road'. This is a short steep climb between houses but very quickly you arc right past the last house to arrive back on the Shire Ditch going north. You may either follow the ridge or the parallel lane (no cars allowed) up to the top of the Worcestershire Beacon. From the lane there is a fine view to the west. Shire Ditch is harder walking and you need to take care not to cause damage, but it does offer a fine view to both east and west. After a couple of stiff climbs you arrive by the **Worcestershire Beacon**.

This 1395ft/425m beacon was erected in 1897 to commemorate the 60th year of Queen Victoria's reign and offers a spectacular panorama in all directions. It overlooks the town of Great Malvern and on a clear day the view extends for miles – the Wrekin (40 miles/64km), Wenlock Edge (33 miles/53km), Long Mynd (38 miles/61km), Edgehill (37 miles/59.5km), Whitehorse Hill (49 miles/79km), the Mendips (62 miles/100km), Broadway Tower (22 miles/35km), Painswick Hill (22 miles/35km) and even the Welsh Mountains. Take time to savour the view your climb has earned.

When ready continue north, now descending. Ahead notice a clear junction of paths with a circular stone waymarker at their centre. Proceed to this and go left descending into the valley past cottages onto a lane which leads down to the B4232 (West Malvern) Road. Cross over the road and follow the sign to the **Brewers Arms** in **West Malvern**. This will lead past the pub – an attractive pub that welcomes walkers. When you are refreshed, continue by taking a path over common land arcing left past houses to Blackheath Way road. Go right along the road and at the first road corner, go left onto a drive towards **Mathon Lodge** Farm. After going through a kissing gate you take a path along a delightful avenue of horse-chestnut trees as you proceed in a general south direction. After passing the farm (to the right) you go over a stile and then take the farm drive to Harcourt Road where you join the Worcestershire Way.

Follow the Worcestershire Way waymarkers by going right and in 40m cross over the road to take a stone track which leads over a pair of stiles. As you follow a clear path to the right of a hedge there is a fine view of the Herefordshire Beacon ahead. Proceed through a gate then enter Park Wood via a stile bearing right onto a wide track called Brockhill Road. The Brockhill Road (no traffic) offers almost a mile of very easy walking and you will be rewarded with glimpses of the Malvern Hills to your left. At the Downs Light Railway (a miniature railway), go left on a path past buildings and through a kissing gate to reach the B4218 road in **Colwall**. Cross over the B4218 and take Broadwood Drive opposite passing by some attractive houses. The drive arcs right as it goes over a railway tunnel. You pass Broadwood House on the left and at the lane corner go through a gate onto a path as you continue along the Worcestershire Way.

Completion of Walks

Proceed ahead, passing through a gateway and at the end of the next field bear left ascending to go over a stile then continuing to the right of the hedge. The path soon veers left as it continues to ascend (the Singing Kettle cafe can be seen up to the left) to a stile into trees. Go right and descend to a stile into open pastureland where once again there are views of the Malvern Hills to the left and the Herefordshire Beacon ahead. The clear Worcestershire Way path arcs to the side of Hanways Coppice which you enter at the second stile. Descend through the coppice eventually exiting via a stile near an attractive cottage called 'Spindrift' – those views are back yet again. Bear left and take the cottage drive until you arrive at the road in **Evendine**. Go right along the road for about 100m then cross over and take the waymarked path opposite. Proceed over a cultivated field and go over a stile as the path continues south over several farm fields. Go over the stile by a permissive path waymarker and go right, walking on the other side of the hedge to a field corner stile. Ignore the finger post going left up to British Camp and continue ahead to a further stile into **Hatfield Coppice**.

Ascend the path through the pleasant coppice proceeding through a gate to reach the busy A449 road. Go left for 20m then cross over the A449 with care and take the Worcestershire Way marked track opposite. Walk past Hill Farm and continue to the right of the Herefordshire Beacon. About 250m past the small farm and just before a gate carrying the Worcestershire Way waymarks, leave the way by going left and commence a zigzag ascent of the **Herefordshire Beacon** for another memorable panoramic view. Initially the view embraces Camp Reservoir and later the main range of the Malverns, including the Worcestershire Beacon

The beacon (1111ft/338m) contains one of the country's finest Iron Age contour forts. The site is believed to have been a fortified hill town of some 2000 people living in timber and mud huts in the third century BC when the natural slopes of the hill were used to advantage in the construction of the defensive ramparts.

After going over the top of the beacon you descend northeast on a clear path (in part with concrete steps to protect the hillside) back to the car park at British Camp.

WALK 44 – Chipping Campden and Dover's Hill

An opportunity to meander the beautiful Cotswold town of Chipping Campden and to enjoy super views over lovely countryside from Dover's Hill.

Distance:	5½ miles (8.8km)
Duration:	Allow 3½ hours
Refreshments:	The Volunteer Inn, Chipping Campden
Walk Start:	Chipping Campden is just over 11 miles (17.5km) south of Stratford-upon-Avon. Calf Lane is to the left below the church
Car Parking:	Park with consideration in Calf Lane, Chipping Campden (GR 152391)
Terrain:	Initially a climb up to Dover's Hill then undulating in parts – all walking is on good footpaths
OS Map:	OL 45 – The Cotswolds

Commence the walk from St James's Church in Chipping Campden. Walk down Church Street and go left along the main High Street which soon becomes Lower High Street and reaches St Catherine's Church. Here, go right and walk up Back Ends, following the Cotswold Way waymarkers. In about 30m bear left up the bridle path of **Hoo Lane** and ascend the gentle slope to the T-junction at **Kingcombe Lane**. Here turn left, cross the lane and then immediately right up a path with the hedge to the right (pausing to look back to see Chipping Campden behind you) until you reach a stile between two ash trees.

Bear left and walk to the top of Dover's Hill to the topograph at its southwest end where you can enjoy the wide view of the escarpment amphitheatre of Dover's Hill and the Vale of Evesham – on a good clear day you can see the Malvern and Bredon hills and in the distance the Shropshire Heights may be seen.

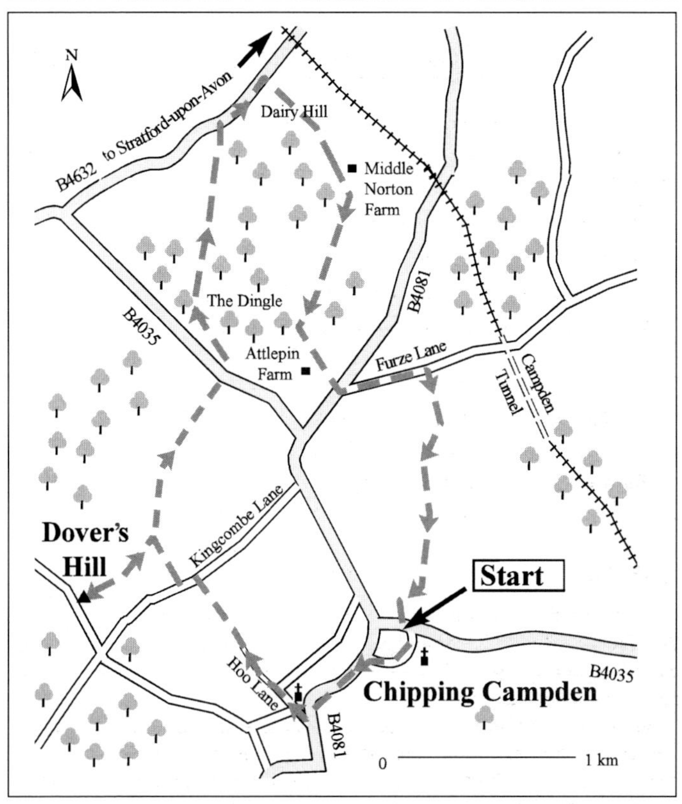

Dover's Hill takes its name from a local barrister, Captain Robert Dover, who in 1612 transformed a small local Whitsunday feast into a grand festival of sport and pageantry which he called the 'Cotswold Olympics' – many centuries before the modern-day Olympics movement. The games are still held on the Friday after Spring Bank Holiday ending with a torchlight procession into Campden. Dover's Hill was rescued from developers in 1920 by Frederick Landscar Griggs who sold out to the historian G M Trevelyan who in turn presented it to the National Trust. The NT maintains Dover's Hill for the general public.

When you have had your fill of the superb view, retrace your steps to the northeast end of the hill and bear left to descend over two fields walking in a generally northeast direction. The view continues to dominate but soon you reach the **B4035** (Aston Subedge to Chipping Campden) road. Cross this road and go through the gate opposite to enter a wood called the **Dingle**, where go left descending the slope on a path which bends right for about 400m to reach a gate. Go through the gate and in 10m go over a stile on the left to walk to the left of a hedge and a stream across two fields to a stile and a copse. Aim for the stile to the left of the copse and go over this onto the **B4632** Stratford-upon-Avon to Broadway road. Go right and ascend this road for 400m then go right onto a bridleway.

Gatehouse to the ruins of Campden House, near the start of the walk

Take this bridleway over several fields with the hedge on your left to reach the top of a hill (known as **Dairy Hill**) and a stile. Go over the stile and continue on a track over fields with trees to your right to a further stile. Proceed diagonally over the next field with **Middle Norton Farm** to your left, aiming for a stile in the far corner. Then continue over three more fields ascending towards the trees, which enter over a cattlegrid. Bear left along the track through the trees and join a metalled road. As you emerge from the trees you pass **Attlepin Farm** on the right to reach the B4081 Mickleton to Chipping Campden road at its junction with Furze Lane.

Cross over the B4081 and follow **Furze Lane** for some 500m. Then go right onto a footpath and proceed over a stile and walk to the right of the hedge to cross a footbridge over a stream. Go diagonally right and follow the edge of the field to some farm buildings, then veer left generally aiming ahead towards the school buildings as you join the Heart of England Way on its route into Chipping Campden. Go right at the end of the school playing fields to take a narrow hedged path along the front of the school. You soon arrive at a kissing gate onto the school road, where go left to reach the **B4035** road by the churchyard. Cross the road and go right along the pavement to return to the church gates from where you started the walk.

WALK 45 – Broadway Tower Walks

Meander the High Street of one of the main tourist towns in the Cotswolds and ascend Broadway Hill to enjoy a very fine view from the famous tower – a major landmark in the Cotswolds. The descent offers a truly wonderful panorama of Broadway embracing the Vale of Evesham, Broadway, Bredon Hill, the Malverns and on a clear day the Shropshire Hills and the Black Mountains.

Distance:	Short walk 3½ miles (5.6km), longer walk 5½ miles (9km)
Duration:	Allow 2 hours for the short walk and 3 hours for the longer walk
Refreshments:	A selection of pubs in Broadway – the Crown and Trumpet near the church in Snowshill Road is a favourite with walkers
Walk Start:	Broadway is 8½ miles (13.6km) southeast of Evesham on the A44 road. Enter the town on the A4632 (Leamington) road just to the north of Broadway
Car Parking:	Pay and display car park (toilets) off the B4632 Leamington road, near the High Street in Broadway (GR 100376)
Terrain:	Hilly but on good footpaths
OS Map:	OL 45 – The Cotswolds

Leave the car park in Leamington Road, Broadway, by the footpath situated immediately behind the toilet block. Cross the alleyway opposite and walk to the main High Street of Broadway. Go left up the High Street, ascending the pavement and passing by some very attractive period houses. Proceed past the last house on the left (Pike Cottage) and continue past the turning circle for cars. About 100m beyond this turning circle, go left towards a road tunnel under the busy **A44** road. Go over a stile and proceed through the tunnel then over a second stile and onto a farm track. Follow the waymark sign to Chipping Campden. This leads up the farm track as it zigzags up the hill. In about 150m go

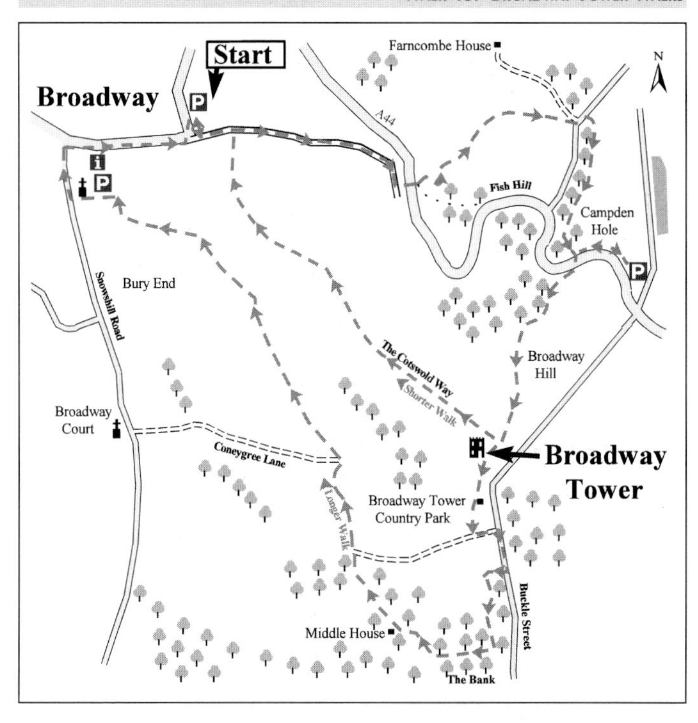

right following the waymark and continue up the hill to reach a path going northeast and then east. You go over a couple of stiles and eventually reach a lane at a junction to the buildings of Group 4 head office. Take time, as you ascend the hill, to pause and enjoy a fine retrospective view of Bredon Hill and the Malverns beyond.

Go over the stile onto the lane and go left for about 10m, crossing the lane and climbing a flight of steps which are cut into the bank. Then go right along the narrow path which runs parallel to the lane. The path winds its way along the edge of the woods of **Campden Hole** passing near to an old quarry. You soon emerge by the A44 road. Bear left to reach the Russell Topograph and if you wish you can continue to a picnic site adjacent to Fish Hill Car Park (with toilets). Pause for a while at the Russell Topograph and enjoy a good view albeit restricted by the trees, then follow the Cotswold Way waymarkers to return to the A44 road on **Fish Hill**.

Broadway Tower

Cross over the road and follow the Cotswold Way waymarkers to Broadway Tower. Initially there is a short bank ascent to join a track bearing right along a narrow path into woodland and then a stile leads to pastureland. Bear right and walk by a hedge to a gate set in lovely new Cotswold stone and this will let you onto a clear footpath over open undulating fields – the vista of Broadway Tower will by now be very clear on the horizon. Follow the clear path across the fields and enter the **Broadway Tower Country Park** through a tall narrow kissing gate (breath in) to reach the tower building.

Broadway Tower was built in 1798 by James Wyatt as a landmark folly for the Earl of Coventry. His seat was at Croome Court near Pershore and from the tower he could pinpoint his hunting lodge estate at Springhill. Climb to the top of the 65ft/20m tower (entry fee payable at the tower shop – well worth it) for a superb view of the surrounding countryside from a height of 1023ft/312m above sea level – the second-highest point in the Cotswolds. The view on a clear day embraces the Vale of Evesham, Broadway, Bredon Hill, the Malverns and can extend to the Shropshire Hills and the Black Mountains – truly magnificent.

Short Walk

Leave the tower and the country park by the same kissing gate you entered and go immediately left to descend towards Broadway town, keeping a Cotswold-stone wall on your right over several stiles. You enjoy a panoramic view for much of the hill descent and you can rest at a viewing seat, sited prior to some steps – this offers a fine view of Broadway town, Burhill and the Vale of Evesham towards Bredon Hill.

Continue down the hill to a hurdle and stile. After going over a further stile in the middle of the hedge bear right to yet another stile in the corner of the field – there are orchards on either side. Cross the stream and proceed through a small yard via stiles (some gates may be left open for you) into a narrow lane which leads to **Broadway** High Street. Cross over the High Street and enter the walled pathway which leads to the car park in Leamington Road.

Longer Walk

From Broadway Tower proceed south towards the Broadway Tower Country Park and pass to the right of the complex keeping to the clear footpath. A stile leads you into a field and this you cross to another stile to arrive on a farm drive. Go left up the drive to arrive at a lane called **Buckle Street**. Now go right and follow the lane for about 200m. Go right over a stile where there is a fine view over Broadway and follow the edge of woodland, pausing now and again to enjoy the view. After going over a mid field stile you go over a second stile to enter the woods. Continue south on the clear woodland path which after about 150m bears right and in about 275m you reach a farm lane. Here go right and follow the lane passing by some attractive Cotswold cottages and the back of the superb **Middle House** – there is a fine view of the surrounding area.

Continue past the Homesteads on the right and walk through a small area of tall beach trees to reach a gate onto open land. Go ahead over two more stiles, passing to the left of a cottage and take a clear path to some trees. Here go over a stile and bear right on a track. In a few yards where the track/lane bends left, proceed ahead over a further stile into open fields (do not go left down **Coneygree Lane**). You now have a very fine view of Broadway ahead of you and there follows a long but gentle and pleasant hill descent – pause periodically to enjoy a super view of Broadway as you approach the town. Cross the field diagonally northwest aiming for a small tree on the bank, then go over a stile in the left-hand corner of the field.

Continue in a general northwest direction over four further fields and their stiles – you pass by or through a small marshy area to reach a footbridge. Go over the footbridge and go left to walk by the field hedge going generally west. In about 450m bear right to cross an attractive arched footbridge and then go left through a kissing gate. Now walk through trees to a second kissing gate that leads along the back of the precinct car park. Continue to the Snowshill Road where go right and follow the pavement past the fine church to reach the High Street of Broadway. Go right and walk up the High Street taking time to enjoy looking at the many superb Cotswold-stone buildings which line one of the most photographed streets in the country.

Broadway nestles below the Cotswold escarpment at the foot of Fish Hill and is one of the most beautiful villages in Britain. Its long High Street slopes down through the town widening out to a triangular green surrounded by honey-coloured stone houses, cottages, inns, tea rooms, gift and antique shops. The area was settled by the ancient Beaker people as long ago as 1900 BC and was later occupied by the Romans. From about AD 1600 Broadway became an important staging post on the main coach route between London and Worcester, bringing prosperity to the town which in the 18th century boasted some 33 public houses! The town became a fashionable place for artists and writers. Abbots Grange dating from the 14th century is believed to be one of the oldest buildings in the county; Tudor House dates from 1660 and part of Lygon Arms dates from the mid 16th century.

After following the High Street for some 500m the main road arcs left and becomes Leamington (Stratford) Road. You will find the car park on the right.

WALK 46 – Bredon Hill Walk

This is an exhilarating walk involving an ascent of 753ft/230m to near the top of Bredon Hill and one of the best views in the Cotswolds – an opportunity to walk one of the most beautiful hills on the edge of the Cotswolds. Seek a day of good weather to appreciate a super view of the Vale of Evesham and the Cotswolds – well worth the effort. You have the choice of a short walk or a longer walk to enjoy what many regard as the best hill view in Worcestershire.

Distance:	4½ miles (7.2km) or 7½ miles (12km)
Duration :	Allow 2½ hours for the short walk or 4 hours for the longer walk
Refreshments:	The Star Inn, Ashton-under-Hill (NB. it may be closed in the morning on Mon, Tues and Wed during the winter months)
Walk Start:	Ashton-under-Hill is 6½ miles (10.5km) northeast of Tewkesbury, west of the A46 Evesham road
Car Parking:	Park in Ashton-under-Hill with consideration for local residents (GR 997377)
Terrain:	Hilly on good footpaths
OS Map:	Explorer 190 – Malvern Hills and Bredon Hill

Short Walk

From your car in Ashton-under-Hill, head north up the pavement of the main road through the village for about ½ mile/800m passing attractive half-timbered cottages (some thatched) and noting the white thatched Old Post House on the right. Towards the top of the village, go left and walk up Cottons Lane. After passing a number of country cottages you ascend the drive of **Shaw Green** and can enjoy a nice view over Aston-under-Hill to your left. The drive bends left and then right to go between farm buildings to a gate and a cattlegrid.

Proceed through the gate and ascend a hedged track to go through a second gate before veering right into delightful open countryside. Aim

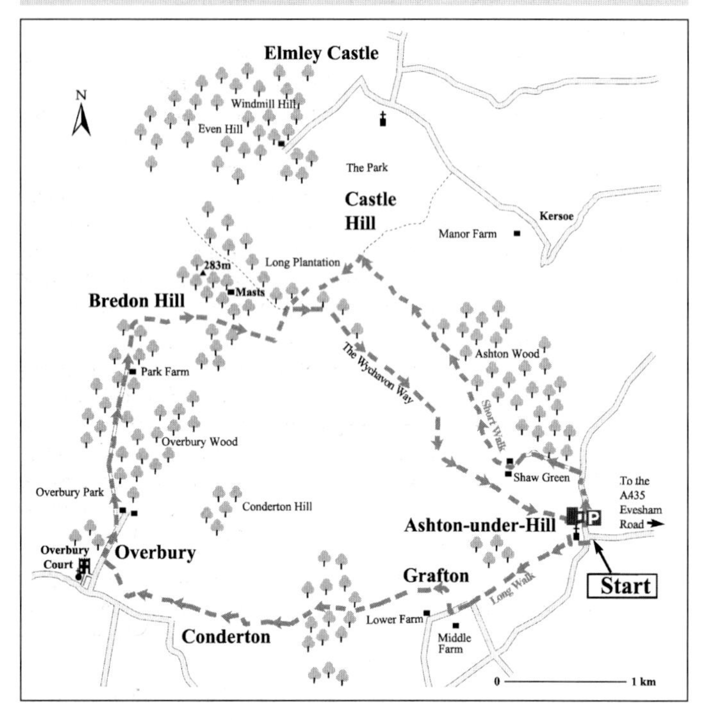

for the gate in the top left corner of the next field then go ahead on the other side of the hedge through a gate to walk to the left of **Ashton Wood** – do this for its whole length, progressing through two further gates. Continue by the hedge in a northwest direction through two gates and then go to the right of the hedge to reach a final gate in the middle of the fence ahead. There are fine views to the right. Proceed ahead over the crest of the hill to go over a stile in the far fence. Then go left to join the Wychavon Way and ascend the slope to a gate into the bottom end of **Long Plantation**.

Ascend through the plantation on a bridlepath track as it weaves its way through the trees to a gate at its very top and the open at 917ft/280m. To complete the walk move forward to **Completion of Walks.**

Long Walk

From your car enter the churchyard of St Barbara's Parish Church in Ashton-under-Hill, leaving it via a kissing gate at the back of the church. Now go left to walk by a pond known as the Moat and to reach a metal gate. Proceed diagonally up the next field aiming for a further gate in the top left-hand corner and onto a lane. Go right along this lane passing a large house which appears to be circled by a superb conservatory, and continue on a wide track with fine views of the Cotswold escarpment and Dumbleton Hill to the left. At the end of the large cultivated field cross a footbridge over a stream and go ahead over the next field to a farm gate set to the right of some cottages.

Proceed onto a lane and follow this for about 200m then go right up a second lane signed 'No Through Road' passing several attractive thatched cottages as you enter the charming hamlet of **Grafton** – a hamlet full of well-tended colourful gardens with a bed of heather at its lane corner. At the end of the lane proceed through a gate signed 'Public Footpath – Conderton' into a large field, initially going to the right of a small fenced enclosure and then aiming for a stile positioned just to the right of the large upper oak tree in the hedge ahead.

Go over the stile and walk towards a further stile into Beckford Coppice – a super bluebell wood. Exit the coppice across some planks over a brook and continue on the clear track to the right of Lower Coppice, crossing over another track and walking by the hedge/wall stile with those fine views to your left. The track bends right around the bottom corner of the next field to go through a gate to the left. Ascend the bank by the fence going over two stiles to reach a lane by the Manor House in **Conderton**.

Bear left and then right (in front of the Manor House entrance) and proceed along the lane to go over a stone stile. Cross straight over the next field to go over a wire fence into a narrow coppice. Walk through the trees bearing right to walk around the fence at the top of the next field, then proceed above this fence on a wide track which takes you behind Overbury Sports Ground and Bowling Green to reach a stone stile onto the road in **Overbury**. Go left passing the Old Police House (on the right) and in 100m go right to the right of St Faith's Church.

Shortly after passing by St Faith's Church, bear right in front of the entrance gates to **Overbury Court** with its fine clock tower and follow

The Savage family memorial in St Mary's, Elmley Castle

Church Row. At its end, go left and proceed up a lane of most attractive houses/cottages with banks of daffodils and forsythia in the early spring. In 400m go left over a cattlegrid into **Overbury Park** and commence a long ascent of about ¾ mile/1.1km up the park road going over two further cattlegrids/gates and eventually joining a farm lane. Pause periodically to recover your breath and to enjoy a fine retrospective view of Overbury and the hills beyond.

Continue up past a turn-off to **Park Farm** and then, at a junction of paths, go right to walk by a lane by a stone wall – from here there is a fine view to the right. The lane becomes a wide track as it progresses east by a plantation of trees with some prominent communication masts to your left. As you proceed beyond the trees a superb view appears to the right over Dumbleton Hill embracing the town of Tewkesbury.

At the field end there is a stone wall, and here you need to bear left and ascend to the left of the wall. You go through two gates and soon reach the edge of Long Plantation near the very top of **Bredon Hill** (283m/926ft).

Completion of Walks

Up to the west is the actual peak of Bredon Hill but you go east, following the **Wychavon Way** waymarkers as you commence a descent of Bredon Hill. The magnificent views from Bredon take in a large slice of the Midlands, and in clear conditions the Welsh mountains can be seen. The summit is a magnificent viewing point and it is not surprising that it was used as a fort in prehistoric times.

Bredon Hill is set on the northwest edge of the Cotswolds and is a landmark of the Midlands and Vale of Evesham. It has an 18th-century tower known as Parson's Folly which sits on its top and is surrounded by a circle of attractive villages.

You follow a clear waymarked path for about ¾ mile/1.2km, initially between the plantation and a wire fence and then passing through a gate by the end of the plantation and continuing to the right of a stone wall and bearing right onto a bridleway signpost. Go through a gate and descend between the hill banks to a waymarker bearing slightly right to reach a metal gate – the views remain superb all the way down the hill.

Descend the next field to go over a stile, maintaining your direction line to go over a further stile. Proceed over the middle of the next field going past two solitary trees to a signpost, then descend steeply towards the church in Ashton-under-Hill, crossing a track before going over two stiles. Continue towards St Barbara's Parish Church and a kissing gate in the bottom left-hand corner of the field. Enter the churchyard, exiting via the fine lychgate to go left and return to your car – you may wish to visit the Star Inn for refreshment.

WALK 47 – Adlestrop and Chastleton House

A pleasant walk in the Evenlode Valley area passing by three superb churches and a fine 17th-century mansion. The village of Adlestrop is a delight and there is the opportunity to visit the National Trust property of Chastleton House.

Distance:	6 miles (9.6km)
Duration:	Allow 3 to 3½ hours
Refreshments:	Nearest pub is at Lower Oddington
Walk Start:	Adlestrop is 6 miles (9.6km) southeast of Moreton-in-Marsh to the right of the A44 Chipping Norton road
Car Parking:	Village car park in Adlestrop next to the village hall – donations (GR 242273)
Terrain:	A walk over undulating land on good footpaths
OS Map:	OL 45 – The Cotswolds

Leave the village hall car park in Adlestrop by going left and immediately left again to follow a signed footpath at the side of the village hall. This is a wide track which passes a horse riding area on the left to go over a stile at the end of the meadow. Proceed on a path aiming for a stile/gate in the far corner of the next field. In a few yards go left over a further stile and then right to follow the right-hand hedge of the next field to reach another stile in its far right corner – you will see the ruins of Hill Barn up the hill to your left. Proceed diagonally and ascend the next field to a stile set in trees in the top left-hand corner and here pause to enjoy a fine retrospective view of Broadwell and the hills surrounding the Evenlode Valley.

Continue to ascend on a brown track through the trees and follow a clear path over a cultivated field to go over the brow of the hill – there is a pleasant view of the surrounding hills – to reach the left-hand corner of **Peasewell Wood**. At the field end, go through a metal gate with a blue waymark and take the clear path down to the road in **Chastleton**. Go right along the road and you are soon in front of the

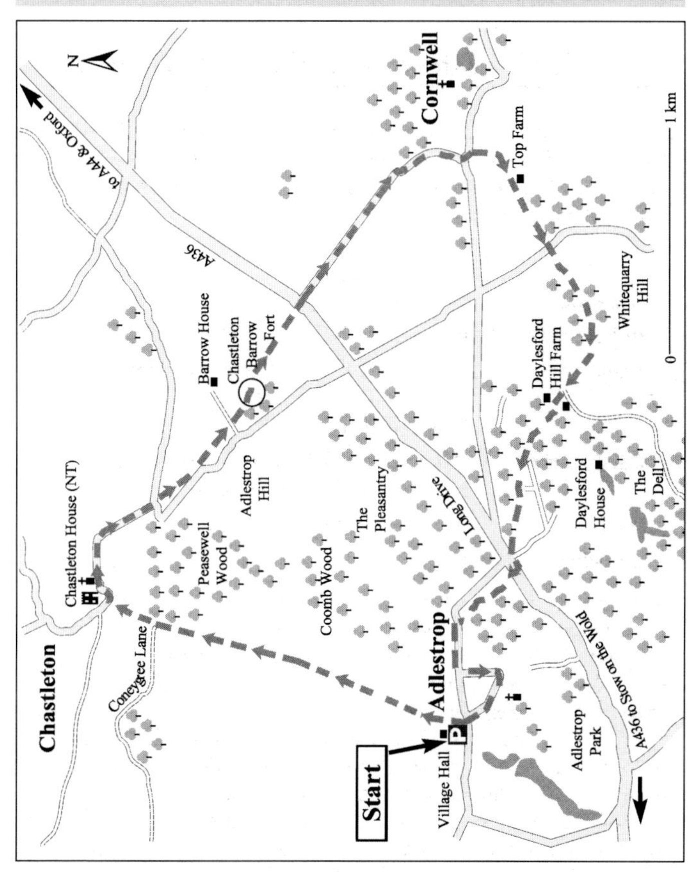

impressive fortified **Chastleton House** with Chastleton's St Mary's Church by its side.

Chastleton House is a fine Jacobean mansion which was built in the early 17th century (it dates from 1603) by a local wool merchant who purchased the estate from Robert Catesby of Gunpowder Plot fame. The building keeps a secret room within its massive walls where a fugitive from the Battle of Worcester hid.

Chastleton House (National Trust)

The mansion has fine panelling and furniture, with outstanding features such as the Great Hall and the Long Gallery on the top floor, which has a magnificent ceiling. It has a fine topiary garden. This National Trust owned house dominates the scenic village of Chastleton.

When you are ready continue along the road going generally southeast and in about 600m you reach a sharp bend in the road. Here continue ahead over a cattlegrid then go through a hand-gate to the right to walk up the right-hand side of a large field. Initially, the path goes by a wall near the lane to some trees and then reaches a gate onto the farm drive, with **Barrow House** on the left.

Cross over the drive and proceed through two more gates, going over a field and through a further gate to enter the Iron Age fort of **Chastleton Barrow** – a pleasant sheltered spot for refreshment if you have some with you. Continue to a final gate on the far left-hand side of the barrow and take a clear track by the left-hand hedge of a field to reach the busy A436 road.

Cross the **A436** and take the lane opposite – signed 'CORNWELL Single Track Road.' This is a quiet lane (seemingly constructed for farm tractors) which descends gently for about ¾ mile/1.4km into the village of Cornwell. As the lane bends right the village comes into view and just after passing trees on the left, go left along a footpath (signed 'To the Church') which initially bisects an orchard and then after going over two stiles becomes a metal-fenced path to Cornwell's tiny St Peter's Church. When you retrace your steps from this pleasant detour you will enjoy a nice view of the 18th-century manor house and its gardens. Back at the lane, go left to descend through the attractive village of **Cornwell** where a small stream is a feature of many of the village gardens.

Cornwell is a tiny backwater village which is more like a serene hamlet than a village. The manor house and many of the village buildings were restored or smartened in the late 1930s and early 1940s by a wealthy American lady who bought the estate. She employed the well-known Welsh architect Clough Williams-Ellis, renowned for his Italian-style village Portmeirion in North Wales.

Continue until you reach a road which cross and proceed ahead to ascend a lane/track which leads to **Top Farm** – with its front garden a blaze of magnolia bushes in the spring. Take the track to the right of the farm buildings to go through a gate and to ascend past trees to a gate onto a lane. Cross the lane and go left for 10m and then right through a further gate to take a most attractive bridleway path that passes through a new plantation containing a number of ornamental trees. Enjoy the view of the Evenlode Hills and Valley to the left.

At a farm track go right and walk between the buildings of **Daylesford Hill Farm** with its attractive flower tubs apparently on parade. Continue on the wide track through trees to reach a stile where you leave the track to follow pastureland aiming for a further stile into woodland in the top right-hand corner of the field. Go over the stile into the woodland and follow its path to reach a gate onto the **A436** road.

Cross the road with care and go past the lane signed to Adlestrop. In 30m go right over a stile and take a clear path through a strip of trees by the side of the lane – this is a pleasant walk through mainly blackberry and holly bushes with a fine view of Adlestrop through the trees to the left. Go over the stile at the end of the tree strip and go left to descend towards **Adlestrop**. In about 100m go left and take a lane through the village where you can visit the church and admire a number of thatched Cotswold-stone cottages.

Adlestrop is a quiet unassuming village set in the Cotswold countryside. Once Great Western Railway trains passed regularly through this now peaceful place on their journey between Oxford and Worcester. Today it is famous because of a short poem written by Edward Thomas following an unscheduled stop at the village railway station on 23 June 1914. His poem opens:

Yes, I remember Adlestrop.
The name, because one afternoon
Of heat the express-train drew up there
Unwontedly. It was late June ...

The steam hissed. Someone cleared his throat.
No one left and no one came
On the bare platform. What I saw
Was Adlestrop – only the name

Jane Austin's uncle (Theophilus Leigh) was the village rector from 1718 to 1762. She visited the 17th-century rectory (now Adlestrop House) in 1806 when she heard that he had inherited Stoneleigh Hall. The Church of St Mary Magdalene is a fine building and contains monuments to the Leigh family.

You emerge at a T-junction where a small bus shelter houses the village name in the form of the old railway station sign. The car park is to the left opposite.

Walk 48 – Tewkesbury Abbey and the River Severn

A meander through history around beautiful Tewkesbury. The walk will take you across parkland by a delightful stream, through a historic battlefield and over a picture postcard golf course for some fine views. The charming village of Deerhurst adds a chapter of ancient history and then a stroll along the banks of the River Severn will return you to Tewkesbury to admire the superb abbey and the town's many places of interest.

Distance:	6 miles (9.6km)
Duration:	Allow 3 to 3½ hours
Refreshments:	Many tea rooms and pubs in Tewkesbury
Car Parking:	Pay and display long stay car park at the rear of Tewkesbury Abbey in Tewkesbury (GR 892324)
Terrain:	Generally easy walking on good footpaths with a couple of undulations
OS Map:	Explorer 190 – Malvern Hills and Bredon Hill

Leave the car park and bear left to go through a kissing gate onto a stream-side path through a recreation park at the back of the famous abbey. The path arcs gently right as it follows the stream to reach and go through a second kissing gate to the left of a bridge to arrive at the A38 road. Cross over the **A38** with care and follow **Lower Lode Lane** opposite.

In about 400m go left at a battlefield waymark onto a clear footpath. This leads across **Bloody Meadow**.

*In **Bloody Meadow** on 4th May 1471 large numbers of Lancastrians were killed by Yorkists as they tried to cross the River Swilgate – the brook is said to have run red with blood. Prince Edward was killed in the retreat in this War of the Roses. The victims of the battle are still remembered in a commemoration service in the abbey on 4th May each year.*

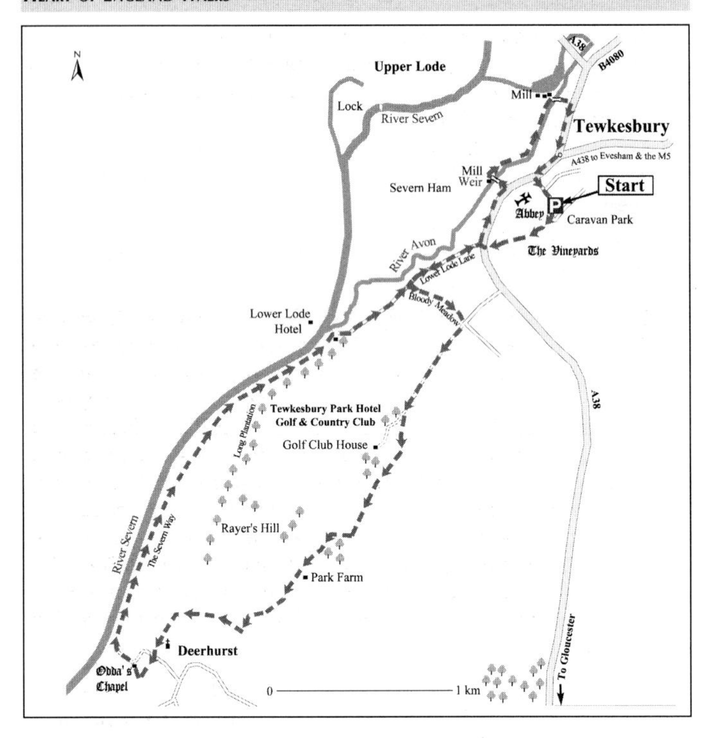

In 300m you arrive at a lane. Go right and take the lane into the entrance drive to **Tewkesbury Park Hotel Golf and Country Club**. Ascend the drive between the golfing areas for some 600m then bear left (south) aiming for a gap in the hedge, where go right and follow the waymarked course edge. This is very pleasant walk and the **Golf Club House** is to the right. You pass by the driving range and cross a fairway en route to a stile into agricultural land.

Once over the stile bear left (southwest) and take the hedge path which arcs around a small area of trees, continuing past **Park Farm**. Maintain the southwest line to go over a stile set in the hedge just past the farmhouse. Now go right and follow the right field edge going over a stile as you descend, with Deerhurst Church tower showing in a group of trees ahead. Proceed around the field edge to go over a stile by a tall tree stump then aim for a waymarked footbridge to the right (in a general northwest direction). Go over the footbridge and continue ahead for a further stile. Take the path which arcs left past a large farm barn to arrive at a hand-gate at the rear of the Priory Church of St Mary in **Deerhurst**.

Enter the churchyard and spare time to visit and photograph this lovely church.

Deerhurst *means 'wood frequented by deer' and the village was once an early Roman frontier. The church dates back to the time of the priory and AD 804. Ethelric was a major benefactor and he probably was the representative of King Offa at the Imperial Coronation of Charlemagne in AD 800. Deerhurst became an important Hwiccian monastery. The monastery's decline was hastened when King Edward the Confessor gave it to the great Abbey of St Dennis in Paris. By 1100 its pre-eminence was overtaken by other abbeys in the area including Tewkesbury of which it became a cell in 1440. It has retained its superb 70ft/21m high tower and the adjacent Priory Farm House. Spare time to view the many ancient features – there is detailed information inside the church.*

Exit the churchyard via its front gate and cross the village lane to go over the waymarked stile opposite. Bear right and go right again at the field corner to reach a stile set to the left of **Odda's Chapel** and Abbot's Court.

Odda's Chapel *(owned by English Heritage) is one of two pre-conquest chapels set in the same village as a Saxon church – the other is in Heysham in Lancashire. The chapel's original dedication stone is now preserved in the Ashmolean Museum at Oxford – it was found in 1675 in an adjoining orchard. There is a reproduction in the chapel which translates to:*

> *'Earl Odda ordered this royal chapel to be built and dedicated in honour of the Holy Trinity, for the good of the soul of his brother Elfric, who died in this place. Bishop Ealdred dedicated it on 12 April in the*

fourteenth year of the reign of Edward, King of the English [1056].'

Continue by going through the gate near to the chapel and take the clear track to reach the banks of the superb **River Severn**. Go right and follow the riverside path towards Tewkesbury. You go through a couple of hand-gates and see a number of motorboats on the river and fishermen on the landing stages. This is peaceful walking and soon you have a deciduous tree plantation to the right. After following the path for about 1½ miles/2.4km you enter a boathouse area via a metal gate. On the far bank is **Lower Lode Hotel** with colourful motorboats moored on the Severn.

Proceed past the boathouse going through a gate and veering right to ascend Lower Lode Lane. At the top of **Lower Lode Lane** go left and follow the pavement of the Gloucester Road (A38) into Tewkesbury with the view of the superb abbey becoming ever more prominent to the right. When by the abbey go left and take the picturesque Mill Street to reach an old **mill**. Cross over the footbridge over the River Severn. Now go right and take the paved footpath above the river, but do pause to enjoy a very fine retrospective view of the mill, the surrounding old buildings and the imposing tower of Tewkesbury Abbey.

The path walk is very pleasant with a selection of colourful moored motorboats as you approach a green footbridge sited just before another large **mill**. Cross over the footbridge and ascend the lane opposite, by the side of a Somerfields store, to reach the High Street facing the Bakers Oven. Go right and take the High Street, passing by the Tudor House Hotel and the Town Hall to reach the main road junction in the town. Go right and follow the pavement of Church Street, noting the many superb timber-framed buildings – Warwick House, the Berkeley Arms and Abbey Cottages. When by Mill Lane, go left past The Crescent into Gander Lane and spare time to visit the wonderful abbey before returning to the car park.

Tewkesbury Abbey *– St. Mary's Church was consecrated in 1121 and is said to be the second-largest parish church in England. It has the highest Norman tower and is larger than 14 cathedrals in*

Tewkesbury Abbey

the country. A home to a Benedictine community of monks for some 500 years it contains monuments to the great families of the Middle Ages and displays some wonderful 14th-century glass.

WALK 49 – Winchcombe and Sudeley Castle

A short stroll from Winchcombe to pass by beautiful Sudeley Castle and then a walk over the nearby hills for some fine views. The walk offers the opportunity to visit the castle and to meander through the fascinating old streets of the attractive Cotswold town of Winchcombe.

Distance:	3 miles (4.8km) or 8 miles (12.8km)
Duration:	Allow 2 hours for the short walk or 4 to 4½ hours for the longer walk
Refreshments:	The Plaisterer's Arms in Winchcombe
Walk Start:	Winchcombe is on the B4632 road situated 10½ miles (17km) northeast of Cheltenham
Car Parking:	Pay and display car park (toilets) in Back Lane, Winchcombe, behind the town library (GR 023284)
Terrain:	Generally easy walking on good footpaths but with a few undulations
OS Map:	OL 45 – The Cotswolds

Leave the car park in Back Lane, Winchcombe, and walk down Cowle Lane to cross High Street and enter Castle Street. Proceed down Castle Street, crossing over the River Osbourne and going right through a kissing gate into parkland to the front of **Sudeley Castle**. You pass right in front of the beautiful castle buildings.

Sudeley Castle *is a historic castle which offers a fascinating story of royal connections spanning some 1000 years. Royal visitors include Henry VIII, Anne Boleyn, Lady Jane Grey, Elizabeth I, Charles I and Prince Rupert. The castle was once the palace of Queen Katherine Parr, Henry VIII's sixth wife. She died of puerperal fever in 1548 and was buried in the castle chapel – Queen's Garden, the centrepiece of the magnificent gardens, is named after her. Cromwell's army desecrated the chapel and caused extensive damage to the castle which at the time of the Civil War was regarded as a top prize.*

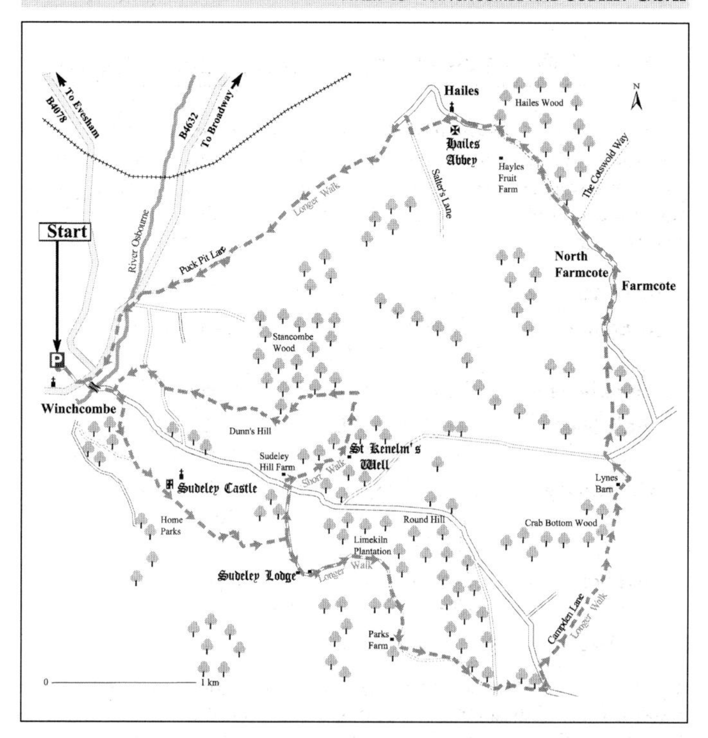

Continue on the path as it veers right and continues through a second kissing gate. Proceed to a gate over the entrance road, passing by an adventure play area. Go right through a metal kissing gate near the front of the castle and then a further metal kissing gate into pastureland known as the Home Parks. Proceed diagonally (southeast) across the **Home Parks** field to its far corner, aiming to the left of an old dead tree with a footpath sign on it. As you cross the field, pause to admire the fine castle.

Climb the stile in the corner of the field and a second stile to the left into the next field, then proceed up the left side of this field to its corner to go right to the far corner and a footbridge/stile. Cross this and ascend the left side of a field to a gate onto a lane.

Sudeley Castle

Short Walk

Go left along the lane and enjoy a fine view of the castle and the surrounding countryside. At the T-junction with the Winchcombe–Guiting Power road, go left then right to walk towards **Sudeley Hill Farm**. Go right over the stile at the farm drive entrance and take the line of the finger post to proceed diagonally over two fields ascending northeast. The footpath veers north just after it enters a third field where it follows the hill contours. Pause to visit the small building of **St Kenelm's Well**. Take time to read the fascinating story that is revealed on the plaque inside the building. Today the intriguing building is little more than a pump house for the nearby farm.

Proceed along the track to the gate at the field end and continue with a steep ascent of a sheep field towards a gate at its top. Before reaching the actual top there is an earlier gate. Go left in front of this and walk below the hedge beneath **Stancombe Wood** for a pleasant descent over two stiles to a field gate – there are fine views over the surrounding Cotswold countryside. Proceed by the edge of the wood to a further gate on **Dunn's Hill** and go through this to enjoy a super view over Sudeley Castle and soon over Winchcombe.

Descend diagonally over the next field aiming for an orange gas pipe marker in the far right corner. Climb over the fence and take the clear path over three more fields to a gate onto a lane opposite the Rushley House, 1894, and its walled garden. Go right along the lane and in about 120m go left through a kissing gate and diagonally (southwest) across a field to a further kissing gate which leads down a narrow passageway to arrive in Castle Street, Winchcombe. Here go right, ascend the street and return to the car park or enjoy refreshments at the Plaisterer's Arms.

Long Walk

Go right along this lane passing in front of **Sudeley Lodge**, then go left to continue up the tarmac lane which soon curves right below **Limekiln Plantation** and **Round Hill**. Continue along the lane to **Parks Farm** then bear left (east) ascending towards the edge of the Warren Plantation. Ascend onto a stone track to walk by the side of the plantation and to reach a small lane, where go left for 20m. Then go right by a hedge to walk around the edge of a field by the side of Guiting Wood and soon to reach the Winchcombe–Guiting Power road.

Go left for about 100m then go right over a stile onto a track known as **Campden Lane** and follow this in a northeast direction for almost 1 mile/1.6km, initially following the contour of a hill and then descending to the right edge of **Crab Bottom Wood**. Take the track to the right of the wood and as it veers north by **Lynes Barn** you reach a farm lane. Go left onto the lane for about 150m to a T-junction. Cross the main lane and go over the stile opposite onto a path which proceeds north, gently ascending over three fields to again reach the lane. Go left onto the lane and follow this into and past a Norman church as you enter the hamlet of **Farmcote**.

Continue up the lane into **North Farmcote** where go left and descend a clear fenced track in a northwest direction. To your left there are excellent views over the valley towards Bredon Hill and the Malverns beyond. In some ¼ mile/0.4km you enter the edge of **Hailes Wood** as you join the Cotswold Way and descend an old cobbled track through the trees to the road. Follow the Cotswold Way waymarkers going right at the road to walk down to the village of **Hailes**.

Hailes Abbey (English Heritage) was built in 1246 by Richard, Earl of Cornwall and brother of Henry III to fulfil a vow made three years earlier when his ship was floundering off the Scillies during a storm. The Cistercian abbey became a place of pilgrimage when Richard's son Edmund presented a phial said to contain the blood of Christ. However, years later Henry VIII declared the holy relic a fake, and the abbey was closed in 1539. Today it is a fascinating ruin with a story to tell.

Immediately after passing by **Hailes Abbey** go left through the kissing gate and cross a meadow and reach and cross Salters Lane. Go right then left along a bridge lane through a gate. Follow the track, crossing a field to a stile, and continue through two kissing gates and then two further stiles into a short fenced passageway. This leads into **Puck Pitt Lane**.

Walk down the hedged lane for some 800m to reach the main **B4632** Broadway to Winchcombe road. At the road, go left towards the centre of Winchcombe and walk along the pavement into the town. You pass by the town hall as you return to your car.

***Winchcombe** is an attractive old Cotswold town which was once the ancient Saxon capital of Mercia. It became home to the Benedictine Abbey having 'university' status in the 15th century and, before being annexed to Gloucester, was the capital of Wincelcumbeshire. Pilgrims who visited the abbey in the 16th century stayed at the George Inn, now George Mews. Winchcombe was once a flourishing Cotswold town, having several streets of stone and half-timbered buildings and retains much of its historical charm. St Peter's Church was built in 1470 and is well known for its 40 grotesque gargoyles – it was a 'wool' church and has an imposing perpendicular tower. The stocks have holes for seven limbs – one hole was apparently intended for a one-legged rogue who lived in the town. In the 17th century tobacco was grown illegally and the townspeople fought the King's soldiers who came to destroy it. Today the town is friendly to all visitors and there are several good pubs, which welcome walkers who can quench their thirst – the medieval George Inn is of particular interest.*

WALK 50 – Blenheim Palace Walk

A pleasant stroll in attractive Oxfordshire countryside ending with a walk up to the magnificent Blenheim Park to see the Column of Victory and to view the famous palace across the artificial lakes introduced by Capability Brown. The walk offers the opportunity to visit the famous Blenheim Palace.

Duration:	5½ miles (8.8km)
Refreshments:	Allow 3 hours
Walk Start:	Various tea rooms and pubs in Woodstock. On returning to Woodstock you will find the Black Prince Inn on the A44 road
Walk Start:	Woodstock is 7½ miles (12km) northwest of Oxford on the A44 road. Hensington Road is to the right as you enter the village
Car Parking:	Hensington Road car park (free with toilets) in Woodstock (GR 446168)
Terrain:	Generally easy walking on good footpaths
OS Map:	Explorer 180 – Oxford, Whitney and Woodstock

Exit the car park in Hensington Road at its rear and go right at the back of houses to reach a road junction. Here go right and take a metalled lane at the back of more houses as you head generally north past the Woodstock cemetery. Where you pass by the sewage works the lane becomes a hedged path as it weaves northwest. After walking the path for about 1 mile/1.4km you go through a gate onto the **B4027** road. Here go left and take the grass verge of the quiet lane up to a crossroads by **Sansoms Cottage**.

At the crossroads go left through a kissing gate on the corner and take the clear path going northwest over a cultivated field to reach and go through a hand-gate. Bear right to go through a further gate then go left over a footbridge and you reach another gate onto open land. There is a pleasant valley view to the right with a pond and the **River Dorn** below – the village of Wooton can be seen on the hill opposite.

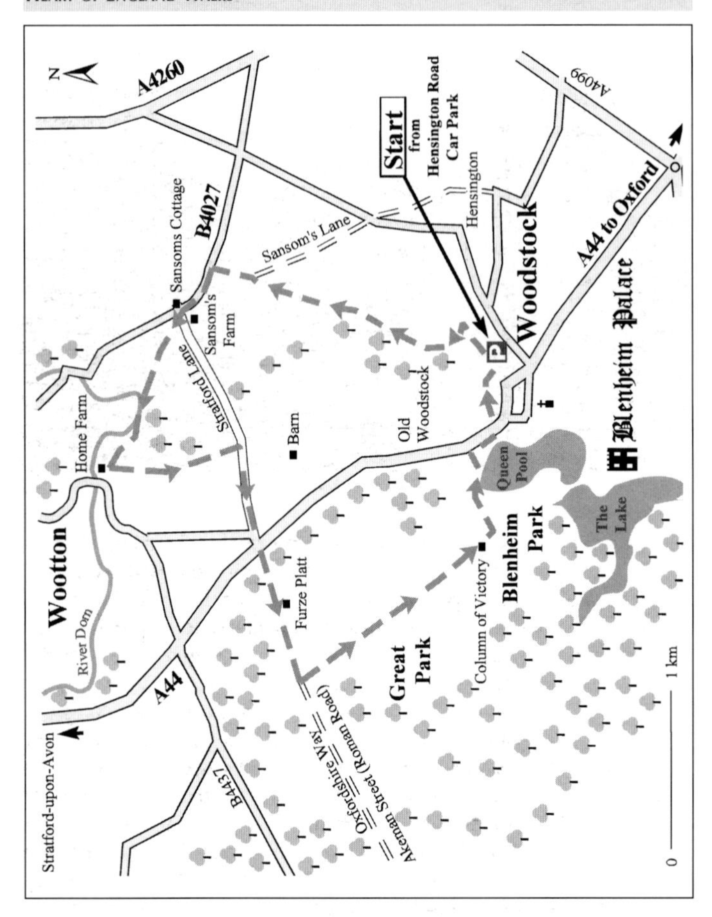

Bear left through a garden to reach a wide track at a junction of paths. Cross over the track and proceed south on a footpath to the right of the field hedge. Maintain this southerly direction over three fields where you will see wild poppies flowering in the summer months. You go over a couple of stiles to reach **Stratford Lane** – it follows the course of an old Roman road and is also part of the Oxfordshire Way.

Blenheim Palace

Go right and ascend the lane until you reach a junction of roads where veer left to reach the A44 road. Cross over the **A44** with care, going through the gate opposite to continue along the Oxfordshire Way in a general southwest direction to a second gate onto a farm track. Go right then left over a stile to follow a clear path which maintains the southwest direction, aiming for a stile to the right of **Furze Platt**. A second stile and a farm gate allow you to stride out along the Oxfordshire Way. About 220m beyond the farm gate, go left and follow (now southeast) a straight tarmac drive up **Blenheim Park** with the **Column of Victory** ahead (erected in commemoration of the Duke of Marlborough's victories over the French) and the impressive north frontage of Blenheim Palace as a backdrop. After ¾ mile/1.1km the drive arcs left and leads down to the edge of **Queen Pool** but you may take the sheep track to closely inspect the huge column and then bear left to reach Queen Pool from where there is a superb view looking towards **Blenheim Palace**.

Blenheim Palace, Sir John Vanbrugh's grandiose masterpiece, was built by John Churchill, 1st Duke of Marlborough, and many famous craftsmen were involved with its construction and ornate decoration. Sir James Thornhill painted the ceiling in the great hall and Rysbrack designed the Duke's monument in the chapel. Capability Brown created the truly magnificent Blenheim Park with its very fine lake. The house was a gift from a grateful nation after the Duke's victory over the French and Bavarians at Blenheim in 1704. Today one of its main attractions is the room where Sir Winston Churchill was born in 1874 – he was the grandson of the 7th Duke of Marlborough. Sir Winston and his parents Lord and Lady Randolph Churchill are buried in the churchyard of the nearby village Bladon.

As you continue above the pool bear left and leave the tarmac drive on a path that leads to a gate to the left of a cottage with a conservatory. Proceed through the gate and you pass between houses to reach the **A44** road in Woodstock. Go right and walk past the Black Prince Inn (perhaps call in for refreshments) and then left over a footbridge onto a clear footpath to the right of a stream.

Although there has been modern development in Woodstock it still retains much of its 18th-century elegance. It is a pleasant village to meander and has a number of antique shops to visit.

Continue on the path as it bears right over a second footbridge and proceed through a gate onto a lane. Go left and ascend the lane for some 300m to a junction. Here go right and you soon find the Hensington Road car park on the left.

OTHER CICIERONE GUIDES

THE MIDLANDS

CANAL WALKS Vol: 2 Midlands ***Dennis Needham***
ISBN 1 85284 225 3 176pp

TWENTY COTSWOLD TOWNS ***Clive Holmes***
Clive describes and draws the most interesting features of these attractive towns.
ISBN 1 85284 249 0 144pp A4 Case bound

THE COTSWOLD WAY ***Kev Reynolds***
A glorious walk of 102 miles along high scarp edges, through woodlands and magical villages by one of Britain's best guide writers.
ISBN 1 85284 049 8 168pp

COTSWOLD WALKS (3 volumes) ***Clive Holmes***
60 walks of between 1 and 10 miles, with local points of interest explained. Beautifully illustrated.
ISBN 1 85284 139 7 (North) 144pp
ISBN 1 85284 140 0 (Central) 160pp
ISBN 1 85284 141 9 (South) 144pp

THE GRAND UNION CANAL WALK ***Clive Holmes***
13 easy stages along the canal which links the Black Country to London. Delightful illustrations.
ISBN 1 85284 206 7 128pp

AN OXBRIDGE WALK ***J.A. Lyons***
Over 100 miles linking the university cities of Oxford and Cambridge. Generally undemanding and easy to follow.
ISBN 1 85284 166 4 168pp

WALKING IN OXFORDSHIRE ***Leslie Tomlinson***
36 walks from all parts of the county, and suitable for all the family.
ISBN 1 85284 244 X 200pp

WALKING IN WARWICKSHIRE ***Brian Conduit***
Attractive pastoral and gentle hill walks include Shakespeare country, the Avon and the Stour. Features many historic villages.
ISBN 1 85284 255 5 136pp

WALKING IN WORCESTERSHIRE ***David Hunter***
Part of the ever growing County Series, this book describes walks for all the family in Worcestershire.
ISBN 1 85284 286 5 200pp 9

WEST MIDLANDS ROCK ***Doug Kerr***
A guide to the popular crags.
ISBN 1 85284 200 8 168pp

DERBYSHIRE PEAK DISTRICT AND EAST MIDLANDS

"Star" FAMILY WALKS IN THE PEAK DISTRICT AND SOUTH YORKSHIRE ***John Spencer & Ann Beedham***
52 short walks adapted from the Sheffield Star Weekend Walk column. 2-3 hours. Ideal for families. Winner of the COLA/OWG Best Guidebook 1998.
ISBN 1 85284 257 1 64pp Wire Bound

HIGH PEAK WALKS — ***Mark Richards***
ISBN 0 902363 43 3 208pp PVC cover

WHITE PEAK WALKS Vol 1: THE NORTHERN DALES — ***Mark Richards***
ISBN 0 902363 53 0 192pp PVC cover

WHITE PEAK WALKS Vol 2: THE SOUTHERN DALES — ***Mark Richards***
ISBN 0 902363 88 3 288pp PVC cover
A best-selling trilogy which covers the most popular walks in the Peak District. Mark Richards' style owes much to Wainwright, but here he proves equal to the master.

WHITE PEAK WAY — ***Robert Haslam***
An 80-mile walk through the Derbyshire Dales with full details of youth hostels, pubs, etc.
ISBN 1 85284 056 0 96pp

WEEKEND WALKS IN THE PEAK DISTRICT — ***John & Anne Nuttall***
12 magnificent circular weekend outings illustrated with John's fine drawings.
ISBN 1 85284 137 0 296pp

WALKING IN PEAKLAND — ***Roger Redfern***
16 original routes to delight the walker and provide an illumination of the features and views encountered.
ISBN 1 85284 315 2

WALKING IN SHERWOOD FOREST & THE DUKERIES — ***Elaine Burkinshaw***
Walking in the heart of England in a rural mix of woodland, farms and parks. For all the family and readily accessible to the industrial midlands.
ISBN 1 85284 279 2 128pp

WALKING IN STAFFORDSHIRE — ***Julie Meech***
40 walks of short and medium length, many in the Staffordshire Moorlands, a remote but accessible section of the Peak District.
ISBN 1 85284 317 9

THE VIKING WAY — ***John Stead***
From Barton-upon-Humber to Rutland Water, through some of the quietest and most attractive scenery in eastern England.
ISBN 1 85284 057 9 172pp